UNLEASHED REDEMPTION

A K9 Handler's Story
of Hope & Healing

David Mendoza III

www.booksforhisglory.com

Unleashed Redemption
A K9 Handler's Story of Hope & Healing

ISBN Hardcover: 979-8-9915151-7-7
ISBN Paperback: 979-8-9915151-6-0
ISBN eBook: 979-8-9922134-0-9

First Edition: January 2025
Edited by Pam Nordberg

Printed in the United States of America

DEDICATION

To my beautiful wife, family, and everyone who has stood by me throughout the years. I am truly thankful for the mentors and leaders that God has brought into my life; their guidance has made my journey so much smoother. Finally, I want to thank our Lord for the joy our four-legged companions bring us. Life would be incomplete without them.

CONTENTS

chapter one

FROM THE BEGINNING

"Before I formed you in the womb I knew you,
before you were born I set you apart;
I appointed you as a prophet to the nations."

JEREMIAH 1:5

The most terrifying words I ever heard in my entire canine career were, "Grab your leash and collar; now go inside that kennel and put it on that shark!" Okay, so it wasn't a shark. In my mind, that's how my future partner appeared to me, for all I could see were his teeth and legs. I didn't know it at the time, but my future partner was a Belgian Malinois, one of the most sought-after work dog breeds to be utilized by law enforcement agencies and militaries around the world.

This was the moment of truth, make it or break it. As I mustered up the courage and stepped into the dog's kennel, all these mixed emotions of fear, excitement, and happiness rushed in. After all the barking, jumping, and wrestling, which seemed like an eternity, I was finally able to place the collar on the dog. I felt this unexplainable sense of accomplishment. The funny thing is, once the collar was on, his expression to me said, "Is that all you wanted from me?"

My childhood aspirations were finally materializing; I was about to embark on a journey as a canine handler with one of the most respected federal law enforcement agencies. As a young dreamer, I envisioned a future filled with possibilities— serving in the military, caring for animals as a veterinarian, pursuing art, or safeguarding my community as a police officer. Although I was uncertain about the timing or the path, from the very beginning I always felt a deep desire to contribute to something larger than myself.

THE FEAR OF GOD

I grew up in the 1980s, in a small town in South Texas. In that area opportunities to succeed were few. Either you adapted to the agriculture lifestyle that several of my relatives followed or took the path of least resistance, "making that easy money" as some called it.

My father had instilled the fear of God in me from a young age . . . or at least the fear of his belt. I would not dare do anything that was against the law or, worse, anything that would tarnish the family name. I respected my dad too much, and besides, even if I tried doing anything wrong, I could never get away with it. You see, the dilemma was, I had a praying grandmother! In case you didn't know it, that is one of the most dangerous weapons that can come against the kingdom of hell. From the beginning I was a marked man—marked by my grandmother's prayers.

My grandmother was an extraordinary woman, the first in our family to embrace Christianity. She embodied her faith in every aspect of her life. Known as a prayer warrior, she dedicated herself to prayer with unwavering commitment. I recall visiting her as a child, often finding her absent. My mother and I would inquire about her whereabouts, and my aunt would simply point to her room and tell us that she was in her prayer closet. There, she would spend countless hours in pursuit of God's presence. When she eventually emerged, her face would radiate with a serene beauty, reminiscent of an angel.

My grandmother's faith was the most profound I've ever

encountered. She never preached from a pulpit or held any prestigious titles, yet she created a remarkable legacy for the family to emulate.

Her devotion to God was evident in her daily life, expressed not merely through her words but through her actions. The love she felt for Christ was infectious; she never pressured anyone to attend church. Instead, others witnessing her relationship with Him naturally inspired them to desire the same connection she had.

One of my most vivid childhood memories is from the time she had her leg amputated due to diabetes. I recall family members gathered around her, questioning how God could let such a thing happen to her. With unwavering faith, she looked them in the eye and said, "God didn't do this to me; I did. But I assure you, when I leave this world for heaven, He will have a brand-new body waiting for me." Those words have stayed with me, leaving a lasting impression. Even today, during tough times, I find strength in her courageous message of hope.

No matter where I went or what I did, I always felt my grandma's prayers over me.

I loved to draw and have always had a love for all animals. And when I say all animals, I mean all kinds. I remember I would carry around a little drawing pad to make sketches of animals every chance I got.

I recall a time back in grade school when I found myself in the principal's office, which happened more often than I care to admit. This visit was due to a peculiar odor that seemed to cling to me. Once I was at the office, the principal decided to call my mother to come to the school and figure out what that terrible smell was. I can still picture my teacher on the phone with her, suggesting she bring an extra pair of jeans, probably thinking I'd had an accident or something.

I still remember the expression on my mother's face when she arrived at the school: a mix of concern and disbelief that seemed to say, *What trouble have you gotten into now, David?* When the school staff asked her to check on me, her surprise was evident as she patted me down and discovered a rolled-up rag tucked in my front pocket. But the real shock came when she unwrapped that rag to reveal a dead mouse inside—yes, a dead mouse!

Now, why would I carry around a dead mouse in my pocket? Well, as I mentioned I love all kinds of animals. So, this little fellow had been trapped by one of the many mousetraps that my father had set out in our home. When I came across it, I thought it looked so helpless and defenseless, so I did what any other five-year-old would have done. I kept it warm and gave it a new home, in my front pocket.

As a kid, I had a variety of pets. At one point, I even had a tortoise that I took with me everywhere. Although I had friends, including my cousins, I always felt a distinct bond with animals. They were special companions, offering a listening ear without any judgment or bias.

If you were to ever see any of my childhood photos, you will always find me holding or petting some kind of animal, whether it's a dog, cat, or any other four-legged creature. Oh yeah, and always wearing a cowboy hat.

HEAVEN SENT

The first dog I ever had was a golden Labrador retriever. He showed up at our house all on his own—quite dirty, exhausted, and in need of water. My dad checked for a collar and any type of identification, but he was not wearing one. As we gave him a bowl of water, I did what any animal lover would do—I seized the moment and asked if we could keep him. My dad, being a fair man with a love for animals himself, which I think is where I inherited it, agreed that we could keep him while we looked for the owner. I realized what his words meant: We had a new dog!

I remember my dad telling me not to name the dog and to avoid getting too attached to him. Of course, I didn't listen, and after some time, I finally settled on the most perfect name I could think of for that dog: Lucky!

Lucky and I were inseparable; wherever my younger brother and I ventured, that dog was right by our side. Whether we were wandering through the neighborhood, heading to the nearby canal, or simply having fun in the backyard, Lucky was always there, never straying far from us.

One evening as we were eating dinner, we heard a loud ruckus in the backyard. A couple kids had jumped onto our property to steal some of our stuff. By the time I peeked out the window, all I saw was the back end of those boys and Lucky chasing after them. They did manage to take my dad's favorite cooler and some other junk we had back there. However, that was the last time we ever saw them.

Lucky always had a way of protecting us. I remember one afternoon after school when my brother and I were strolling through the alley, suddenly a stray dog appeared out of nowhere, growling at us. Just then, Lucky sprang into action, charging straight at that dog. My brother and I quickly dashed back home, while Lucky took it upon himself to show that mangy dog who was boss.

One day, after his usual exploration around the neighborhood, Lucky returned home with a noticeable limp. A closer look revealed a nasty wound on his front paw, as if someone had struck him with an axe. My dad did everything possible to care for that injury. Although it eventually healed, Lucky was never quite the same after that. As he aged, I remember the day he simply chose to say his goodbyes and didn't come back. My dad explained that dogs would often wander off to die. Whether that was true or not, I believed it was, because Lucky had always been there for us, and it felt like something he would do on our behalf. He was truly heaven-sent.

Throughout my life, I've had many dogs, but Lucky left a lasting impact on me. I always felt safe when he was around; he not only looked after us but also made me feel like my best friend was always with me.

During my middle school years, a police officer would regularly visit our campus with his trusty detection service canine. Together, they would inspect the lockers for any concealed contraband students might have kept. The officer's partner was a cheerful black Labrador retriever, which brought to mind my own dog, Lucky. This service dog had such a friendly demeanor. Watching this dynamic duo in action made me think, *That's a job I would really love to have.*

THE SHIFT

As I wrapped up my eighth-grade year, I found myself veering off course academically. My focus had shifted from my studies to spending time with friends. That was until a group of visitors arrived, completely transforming my life.

A group of high school students from the United States Marine Corps Junior Reserve Officer Training Corps (JROTC) Drill Team arrived to showcase their skills. As soon as I laid eyes on their sharp-looking dress blues and the flawless precision with which they executed their drills, I was captivated. The highlight was watching an M-14 rifle soar through the air, expertly caught by one of the cadets. At that moment, I realized I had never even heard of the US Marine Corps or the JROTC program before, but I was completely convinced that I wanted to be a part of it.

To join this unit, maintaining strong grades was essential, particularly if you aspired to be on the Drill Team. That year, I scraped through the eighth grade, but a shift had occurred within me. For the first time, I felt an unwavering certainty about my future. Before this, I had dabbled in numerous sports and activities, even participating in band, yet I always felt out of place. This group was unlike anything I had experienced; little did I realize it then, but God was using this experience to completely transform who I was.

The following year, I was thrilled to become a US Marine Corps JROTC cadet, realizing my short-term dream. My primary ambition at that time was to be part of the Drill Team, so I committed myself to not only achieving top grades but also ensuring I kept them up.

As a first-year student, the moment arrived for me to audition for the Drill Team, which was looking to fill two backup positions. The tryout process included standing at attention in the center of the team while they tossed M-14 rifles back and forth. The members would compete to see who could throw their rifle closest to my face and the back of my head at the same time. My task was simple: remain completely still, no matter what happened. If I flinched or moved, I would be disqualified—and likely end up getting hit by a rifle in the process.

When I found out I had made the team, a profound sense of clarity about my future came over me. For the first time, I experienced a feeling of belonging, as if I was finally home. During my high school years, the team competed locally and throughout the state, bringing home numerous trophies and awards. Before this experience, I had never stepped out on my own, but I now understand that this journey was an essential element of God's plan for my transformation. The JROTC program instilled a newfound confidence in me, one that continues to be a vital part of my life today.

I owe a great deal to my mentors from high school JROTC, a retired colonel from the US Marine Corps and a retired gunnery sergeant. Until that time, I had never encountered individuals like the colonel or gunny. They were strict yet always showed respect to everyone. This brings to mind a quote by Johann Wolfgang von Goethe that I noticed on the wall of my first K9 instructor's office. The essence of the quote is, "Treat a man as he is, and he will remain as he is. Treat a man as he could be, and he will become what he should be." Isn't that how God works? Instead of calling people based on their current fallen condition, He calls us from what we'll become, a new creation in Christ.

ANOTHER WAY OUT

As I approached high school graduation, my desire to enlist in the United States Marine Corps was undeniable. Now a junior on the brink of becoming a senior, I decided to visit the Marine Corps recruiter. He informed me that I had the option to enlist a full year ahead of schedule if I chose to. At eighteen, I was ready to take the plunge, so I eagerly asked, "Where do I sign?"

In my thoughts, I envisioned an escape from South Texas, a path toward achieving my dreams. Although my father was a hardworking man, dedicating most of his life to being a mechanic, in my family the pursuit of higher education or a military career was unheard of.

One thing I could always rely on with my dad was, however, that we were never in need. I recall a moment when I was lending a hand to him while he was swapping out a carburetor. My role was mainly to pass him the tools he required. That day, I noticed his hand was covered in blood from where he had struck it against the engine block during the removal process. He glanced at me and asked, "Son, do you know why my hands look like this?" I replied, "Because you hit them, Dad?" He then said, "My hands are like this so yours don't have to be."

That phrase has echoed in my life for as long as I can remember. At first, I didn't quite understand its depth, but the moment I became a father, everything clicked. It took on a whole new level of importance, especially after I embraced my faith as a born-again Christian. During a church service one day, as I pondered my dad's words, the thought suddenly struck me that our heavenly Father made the ultimate sacrifice so that we could be free from the consequences of our sins and able to live for Him in freedom and in truth.

My parents made incredible sacrifices to ensure we had

what we needed, just like so many other loving parents do for their kids. I remember one evening when they were discussing my future. My mother expressed her excitement about what I would become as I grew up, mentioning how wonderful it would be to have a son who could support them financially in their later years. My dad chimed in, saying, "No, dear, our role is to help them thrive." He reflected on how things used to be, when families had many children to assist with farm work, but emphasized that today, a family's focus should be on supporting their children's success.

I truly believe, as parents, our purpose is to create a path for the next generation to thrive. I desire for my children to achieve greater success than I have, not only in terms of finances, education, and careers, but most importantly, I hope they excel spiritually. My heartfelt prayer is for their relationship with the Father to be deeper than mine ever was. In many respects, I find myself sharing the same words of wisdom with my children that my father once shared with me: "My hands are like this so yours don't have to be."

I owe a tremendous debt of gratitude to my parents for equipping me for the challenges that awaited me. Even though they married at a young age, they possessed a wisdom that feels rare in today's world. Life's tough lessons were their greatest educators.

Before I left for the military, my mother made sure I was equipped with essential life skills such as cooking, doing laundry, and ironing. At the same time, my father taught me vital principles such as responsibility and integrity, helping to shape me into a man who honors his commitments. I was not aware of the true value that came behind each chore and responsibility that my parents would have me do during my adolescent years.

Only when I found myself alone did I truly understand the priceless lessons my parents had taught me. During boot camp, while many were grappling with the simple tasks of making their beds, ironing their uniforms, or even just sweeping and mopping, I felt grateful for my parents' guidance, which had given me a solid foundation in these skills.

I have come to realize that our heavenly Father prepares His people much like a caring parent readies their children for what lies ahead. In Psalm 144:1, the psalmist proclaims, "Praise be to the Lord my Rock, who trains my hands for war, my fingers for battle." God equips us not only for the long journey but also for the challenges we face right now. No matter what struggle you are encountering, God has given you the tools to respond effectively. As Christians, we are called to engage in this battle through the power of the Holy Spirit, rather than relying solely on our own strength. It is through our submission and obedience to Him that we will experience true victory in our lives.

BROKEN DOWN TO BE BUILT BACK UP

Many young individuals today join the military mainly to take advantage of the GI Bill. However, when I enlisted, that wasn't my reason at all. I was focused on building a career as a Marine, completely oblivious to the fact that a college degree would be essential for career advancement.

I chose not to take advantage of the GI Bill. During boot camp, a drill instructor approached us recruits and inquired who was interested in signing up for it. While most of my fellow recruits eagerly raised their hands to receive the form he was distributing, I stayed quiet and didn't ask for one.

When the DI reached me, he peered at me as if I were an oddity for not participating. He repeated his question to ensure I understood. With as much respect as I could muster, I replied, "No, Drill Instructor, this recruit is not signing up for the GI Bill." He simply walked away, shaking his head in disbelief.

Looking back now, I truly wish someone had taken the time to emphasize the importance of pursuing higher education after high school. During my deployment, many of my fellow

Marines were able to attend college through correspondence courses, making the most of the GI Bill. At that time, my primary focus was solely on my duty as a US Marine.

Years later, I eventually enrolled in college, but I had to finance it myself, which was a tough lesson to learn. If I could turn back the clock, this is one aspect I would definitely change. Although I made a significant mistake, I believe God turned it into something positive later in my life.

Only a month after I enlisted in the Marines, the first signs of Desert Shield emerged, soon leading into Desert Storm. For us recruits, this signaled that our training was about to intensify. True to form, the drill instructors ramped up the pressure in every aspect of our training. Their mission was clear: to tear us down entirely, only to rebuild us into what they referred to as a "lean, mean fighting machine."

A significant number of individuals dropped out for various reasons. Whether due to health issues or mental struggles, the numbers dwindled with each passing day. I had faced my share of challenges during my upbringing, but nothing—absolutely nothing—could compare to the trials I was enduring at boot camp.

Each day presented its own unique set of trials. I recall a particular instance when the drill instructors had us in the sand, barking orders for us to do push-ups, bends and thrusts, stomach crunches, and a slew of other intense exercises.

The shouts echoed around us, reminiscent of a pack of wild dogs as they kicked sand directly into our faces, making it nearly impossible to focus. I couldn't help but wonder, *What in the world is wrong with these guys?* We were trying our best to follow their commands, yet instead of allowing us to finish the job, we were met with sand in our faces. What was the purpose of that?

The more effort we put in, the more our drill instructors seemed to challenge us. The shouting, the relentless marching, the endless push-ups—none of it registered in my fading civilian mind. We were thrown into all sorts of wild situations, yet strangely, the more we endured, the more we began to appreciate the difficulty. As the days went on, conditions became harsher, but somehow, it all felt more manageable.

One of the most motivating drill instructors we encountered was a Recon Marine. He pushed us in ways that no other DI could. His approach to inspiring us was unique, characterized by a heartfelt and authentic connection with his recruits.

He was the type of leader who motivated you to exceed your own expectations, encouraging you to complete more push-ups than you ever thought possible. He challenged us to go beyond our limits, and we welcomed it. What made his leadership even more special was that he often joined us on the floor, doing push-ups side by side with us.

This same DI sported a striking tattoo on his calf that depicted a Marine drill instructor shouting at a recruit struggling through push-ups accompanied by the words "Pain is merely weakness leaving the body." And yes, his calf was impressively large. This brings to mind the verse from 2 Corinthians 4:17, which states, "For our light and momentary troubles are achieving for us an eternal glory that far outweighs them all."

WORTH THE PAIN

After countless hours of hard work and emotional challenges, the moment had finally arrived. I was about to earn a title that few possess, that of a US Marine. All those long days and sleepless nights had culminated in this achievement. The feeling was beyond words, but the honor was not mine alone. The collective triumph was shared with my fellow Marines who stood by me, owing a great deal to our drill instructors who pushed us beyond our limits, ensuring we were ready for whatever lay ahead.

Soon after completing Marine Combat Training, we were

assigned to our new training units, with our Military Occupational Specialty (MOS) guiding our placements. Several training facilities had been closed temporarily due to the Marine instructors being deployed. True to the Marine Corps spirit, we adapted, overcame, and focused our efforts at the facilities that were still operational.

Many of us found ourselves being shipped off from California to North Carolina. With the war still raging, our MOS training was cut short, but we got the essential skills we needed before being sent directly to the fleet. Upon arriving at our assigned units, we discovered that half of our company had already been deployed.

Just a few months after I arrived, our unit received orders to head out to an active conflict zone. On this, my first deployment outside the United States, we were on a humanitarian mission. I ended up spending around six months on that mission. To my surprise, as soon as I returned to the US, our unit was sent out again almost immediately. This became a recurring theme throughout my Marine Corps career—constant back-to-back deployments.

This situation wouldn't have been as challenging if not for my new bride. We got married right after I completed my MOS training, and we were both incredibly young. It hardly seemed fair to her, but I felt the Marine Corps was a necessary step for our future. Balancing marriage with deployments is undoubtedly one of the most difficult circumstances anyone can face.

I spent my final year in the Marine Corps stationed in Okinawa, Japan. Honestly, if not for the deep connections I formed with my fellow Marines, the experience would have been incredibly challenging. Many people claim that a visit to Okinawa transforms you into either a devout believer, a social drinker, or a fitness enthusiast. Personally, I feel like I emerged from that experience embodying all three. At that time, my connection with my heavenly Father was superficial; it was more of a religious trend driven by circumstance than a genuine faith.

Reflecting on those years, I realize that the shouting, the many push-ups, the hard running, the marching with heavy packs, and the intense stress all had a bigger goal. The military was instilling in us a resilience that no one could ever strip away—the invaluable skill of perseverance.

Despite the numerous challenges I encountered during my time in the Marines, I wouldn't alter a single moment. Even now, I continue to draw strength from those experiences to propel myself forward. I believe these moments were part of a greater plan teaching me to place my trust in God's will rather than relying solely on my own abilities.

chapter two

NO GREATER BOND

"Two are better than one, because they have a good return for their labor."

ECCLESIASTES 4:9

The end of my four-year service in the Marine Corps had arrived. I found myself considering the possibility of reenlisting, but I realized this decision wasn't solely mine to make. To approach this matter properly, both my wife and me had to come to a mutual agreement about potential reenlistment. I understood that I was no longer acting as an individual; our lives were now intertwined as a team.

I remember making a call to my wife from a pay phone in Okinawa, Japan, seeking her thoughts on my decision to reenlist in the Marine Corps. I can still hear her voice encouraging me to return home and chase my long-awaited dream of becoming a law enforcement officer.

Her words resonated deeply with me; they signified not only her desire to have me nearby but also her understanding of my inner aspirations. I am truly grateful to my Lord for the wisdom my wife shared that day. Thanks to her, my path shifted toward a brighter future.

The long-awaited day to return home had finally come. After spending nearly a month at Camp Pendleton, California, navigating the process of separating from the Marine Corps, I was ready to head back. With a one-way ticket in hand, I arrived at Dallas International Airport, only to realize I had lost my boarding pass. It dawned on me that I had left it tucked in the back of the front seat on my previous flight. In a rush, I dashed back to the old gate, but by the time I arrived, the cleaning crew had already cleaned out the entire plane.

I found myself in the position of needing to buy a new ticket home, using up the little savings I had managed to set aside. Upon my arrival at my hometown airport, I was met with an empty terminal—no one was there to greet me. Apparently my wife's car had broken down on her way to pick me up. This was back in the days before cell phones, making it nearly impossible to reach anyone. We had our own inventive methods for communication, usually calling relatives in the hope of finding each other, but it often took a while for the message to be relayed.

I spent around an hour waiting, reaching out to every one of my wife's relatives whose numbers I had. Eventually, I made the decision to rent a car, further depleting my savings. I set off toward her hometown, where she lived with her parents since we'd not had a chance yet to establish a home together, hoping I would run into her on the way. Little did I know, her aunt and uncle had already taken the car to a repair shop and given her a lift to the airport.

A few hours later, we finally reunited at her cousin's place. The joy of seeing each other was overwhelming, almost like a dream. The moment we had both been waiting for had finally come. We spent the remainder of the day catching up, swapping stories, and reminiscing about the wonderful times we had shared in the past.

READJUSTING

After being away for four years with taking only short leave in between deployments, I returned to find everything transformed. My hometown, which was an hour away from where I now lived with my wife and her parents, looked different, and the familiar surroundings felt foreign. Even within myself, I sensed a shift. Visiting my parents' old house or the spots where my friends and I used to gather, I couldn't shake the feeling that nothing was as it once was.

Many of my high school friends had moved on by then, so I felt like an outsider. No matter where I turned or what I engaged in, I struggled to find my place. Even with my wife, I felt a sense of distance.

I couldn't seem to relate to anyone. Although I had eagerly anticipated returning home, it no longer felt like the place I remembered. I often caught myself longing to be back in the Marine Corps, deployed alongside my fellow Marines. The camaraderie we shared was unlike anything I had experienced before; it was a bond forged in the heat of adversity, built on trust and mutual respect.

In the field, every day was a challenge, but it was a challenge we faced together, side by side, with a shared sense of purpose. The adrenaline of missions, the late-night conversations under the stars, and the unwavering support we offered one another created a sense of belonging that I now craved deeply.

Adjusting to civilian life was quite challenging. There were no resources or training available to help ease the transition. I was not only dealing with the pressure of searching for a new job while being unemployed, but I also found myself mentally unprepared for the abrupt changes that occurred. I noticed that I rarely ventured out anymore. Even when I did go out with my wife, the experience felt different; I was constantly on edge.

Whenever we settled into a restaurant or any public place, I felt the need to keep an eye on all the exits, ensuring I was positioned to see them. No matter where I was or what I was doing, my mind was preoccupied with worst-case scenarios, and I found myself unconsciously devising plans to handle them.

I turned to excessive drinking as a way to numb the pain of reality. I felt utterly lost in my battle against the loneliness and chaos that overwhelmed me. God seemed to have vanished from my life, even though I recognized that I had been the one to distance myself from Him. Deep inside, I understood the solution; my grandmother had imparted that wisdom to me since I was a child. Still, I wrestled with the thought of reaching out to God, fearing it would make me a hypocrite.

I believed that going to God would just be a way for me to seek a quick fix. That wasn't what I wanted; I valued true commitment. At that moment, I felt unprepared to embrace such a commitment, or so I believed.

I pressed on, pushing through as we were taught in the Marines. I had mastered the art of concealing my pain, burying it deep within so that no one else would feel its weight. What I failed to realize was that by keeping my feelings to myself, I was damaging my marriage even more. My wife and I had become like strangers; the long deployments had driven a wedge between us. The connection we once shared had faded away.

Such a sensation is difficult to articulate. Despite my best efforts to find happiness and make my marriage thrive, nothing seemed to click. I attempted to re-create the passion of our high school romance by planning dinners and dancing, but those evenings often spiraled into arguments. The root of my frustration lay in my struggle to feel like I belonged. I felt like an oddity wandering through an unfamiliar landscape.

To save both my marriage and myself, I knew that change was necessary. What started as a single day stretched into weeks, and those weeks turned into months, leaving my wife and me feeling like we were merely going through the motions.

Eventually, we had the heartfelt conversation we had been yearning for. As my wife shared her feelings, I opened up about everything I had kept bottled up as well. We recognized that we still loved each other, but we understood that moving forward would require us to take things one day at a time and to be mindful of each other's needs.

My relationship with my wife gradually improved. We weren't completely in the clear, but we were both committed to being open with each other. I still felt out of place and had a raging chaos inside me, but at least I had someone by my side.

The pressure was mounting as my savings continued to shrink with each passing day. Although I had been relying on unemployment benefits, they were about to run out. I realized that if I didn't begin my job hunt soon, we would find ourselves in a tough situation.

DEAD ENDS

During that period, while my wife and I lived with my in-laws I desperately searched for a new job, I submitted applications to every law enforcement agency imaginable, both local and federal, but nothing seemed to come through.

Although my lifelong aspiration was to become a law enforcement officer, I realized I needed to hit the brakes on that dream for a while. I began sending out applications far and wide. I reached out to large corporations, local shops, and small family-owned grocery stores, all in an effort to get my finances in order. This was back in the days before the internet and computers, so I took the traditional route, making phone calls, applying in person and by mail.

I found that every place I applied to was looking for candidates with a college degree. Even when I highlighted my four years of military service, it didn't seem to make a difference. In a moment of desperation, my wife took a job at a nearby restaurant. This hit me hard; I had always believed it was my responsibility as a husband to be the primary provider for our family.

Throughout my life, I've come to realize the importance of planning. In Luke 14:28, the Bible reminds us, "Suppose one of you wants to build a tower. Won't you first sit down and estimate the cost to see if you have enough money to complete it?" They say wisdom often comes with age, and I can't help but wish that when I was younger I had known even a fraction of what I understand now. I certainly would have approached my plans with more foresight. Before I joined the Marine Corps, I truly believed I was making the right choice to secure a better future for my wife and me.

It certainly didn't seem that way at the time. The regret of not enrolling in the GI Bill loomed over me constantly. I kept sending out job applications, but none yielded any positive responses. The weight of my job search frustration was becoming overwhelming. On the bright side, my wife was contributing financially, which allowed us to assist my in-laws in paying the utility bills and groceries.

One Saturday evening, at a family gathering, one of my wife's cousins came up to me and asked if I was still on the job hunt. I eagerly replied that I was. He mentioned that an oil field company was hiring and suggested I should apply, although it would require traveling out of state every two weeks. Just then, another cousin joined us and told his brother not to be foolish, saying that kind of job wasn't right for me and that I should be in law enforcement or something similar.

I had reached a stage where I was open to any opportunity that came my way. However, the thought of having to travel held me back from applying, as I worried it might negatively impact my marriage rather than strengthen it.

My wife and I faced ongoing financial difficulties, and my unemployment benefits now had run out. I had submitted an application to a cable company for a cable installer position, drawing on my previous experience in the Marines that was relevant to this role. To my surprise, I received a call inviting me for an interview. The best part was that the company was located nearby, making me eager to pursue the opportunity.

HOPE

The next day I received another call from a major grocery store. They wanted to know if I was available to work the midnight shift as a grocery overnight stocker. The pay was comparable to the cable company, so I graciously declined their offer.

A few days later, while I was preparing for the upcoming interview with the cable company, a friend reached out to see if I was still on the job hunt. He informed me that the sheriff's department was actively looking for detention officers and asked if I was interested. I replied that I had already applied but hadn't received any response yet. To my surprise, he insisted that wasn't how things were done in that area. My friend urged me to march myself directly to the sheriff's office, request a meeting with the sheriff, and introduce myself along with my career aspirations.

I wasn't accustomed to handling things like that; it felt like I was undermining the chain of command in numerous ways. Yet, driven by my desperation, I decided to take my friend's advice and act on it. In fact, I headed straight to the sheriff's office that very day.

Upon arriving, I inquired about the possibility of speaking with the sheriff. His secretary asked what the purpose of my visit was. I clarified that I had applied to the sheriff's department and wished to meet the sheriff to ask about several job openings.

I was quite surprised when he consented to meet with me. After about twenty minutes of waiting, I finally walked in to chat with him. I had expected to be greeted by one of the junior deputies—a sergeant, lieutenant, or maybe even a captain— but definitely not the top boss himself.

Instead, I was welcomed by an imposing figure—a tall, broad man with a handshake that could almost crush bones. For a moment, I felt as if I were face-to-face with Wyatt Earp himself. I had encountered my share of tough individuals during my time in the Marines, but this gentleman exuded a unique presence that set him apart.

He invited me to take a seat and immediately inquired about my background and where I was from. I shared that I wasn't local to the immediate area but that my wife's family was. I also mentioned that I had recently completed my service in the Marines and was eager to pursue a career in law enforcement.

Fortunately, the sheriff had a way of speaking that put a

person at ease. He posed a straightforward question: Why did I aspire to join law enforcement? I replied that, with all due respect, I could easily give him a typical response, but I preferred to be honest. I explained that my desire to enter into a law enforcement career stemmed from a deep-seated belief that it was my true purpose. I emphasized that I felt it was my life's calling.

He then clarified that, if hired, I would begin my role as a detention officer on the jail side, and once a patrol position became available, I would be considered for it. He inquired when I could start, and without a moment's pause, I replied, "Today, sir." He responded with a warm welcome, saying, "Very well. Welcome aboard!" Shortly after, he contacted his lieutenant from the jail section to give me a tour and coordinate my schedule.

During my time in the Marines, I had taken on some additional responsibilities as a prisoner escort, known in the field as a "chaser." One of the most challenging moments I faced occurred in Okinawa. When my turn came to serve as a chaser, of all the individuals I could have been assigned to escort around the base and take to the brig, I ended up having to escort one of my close friends from my unit.

This Marine had faced some tough times; he had missed

formation a few times due to overindulging the night before, which led to disciplinary action. The real issue was that this wasn't the first time it had happened.

My friend had discovered that his wife, who was also a Marine, was pregnant with another man's child and wanted to end their marriage. The situation escalated when he broke his restrictions; in a drunken state, he climbed to the roof of a five-story barracks, threatening to jump. The corporal on duty had no choice but to call the military police to intervene.

The following day, I was tasked with escorting him around the base in handcuffs as he completed his outprocessing from our unit. After he went through all the necessary stations, the final destination was the brig. To this day, I can't shake the terrible feeling of having to bring my friend to that place. Once we arrived and I handed him over to the brig officials, they immediately removed his uniform and began to berate him, treating him far more harshly than our drill instructors ever did during boot camp. The final thing my friend said to me was, "I'm really glad it was you who dropped me off."

As I stepped into the jailhouse alongside the lieutenant, this was the memory that resurfaced. My friend and I had faced numerous challenges together during our deployment.

Reflecting on those times, I can't help but feel a sense of regret for not being able to support him more. If only I'd had the deep connection with my Lord that I cherish today.

During my initial walk-through of the jail, I had the opportunity to meet the sergeant, who graciously guided me on a tour of the facility. As we strolled through the halls, he took the time to introduce me to the various detention officers and staff members who made up the team.

However, while we were in the back area, I found myself in an unexpectedly awkward situation. Inmates gathered on the other side of the bars erupted into a loud chorus of catcalls as we passed by. In response, the sergeant's authoritative voice cut through the noise, commanding, "Knock it off!" and just like that, the raucous sounds from the prisoners fell silent.

Following the tour, I was handed my schedule and a uniform shirt. The sergeant locked eyes with me and emphasized, "Never allow any of the inmates to disrespect you; respect is paramount here." He then informed me that I would be starting that night and instructed me to check in with the sergeant on the midnight shift when I arrived. He assured me that he would be expecting me.

When I got home, my wife had just wrapped up her shift at the restaurant. She was eager to hear about my day at the sheriff's office. I excitedly told her the great news that I had landed the job, but I also had to share the not-so-great part: I needed to start the midnight shift that night.

In that moment, our joy completely overshadowed any worries about working late hours. She comforted me by saying she was simply happy to have me nearby. It was nothing like those times when I was away on deployments, feeling isolated without any means to communicate, which made everything so much harder.

A NEW LIGHT

I started my new job with a blend of feelings. On one hand, I was excited to finally be employed, but on the other, I still felt a bit out of place among everyone. However, slipping into that uniform felt great, and the highlight was being able to wear my cowboy hat with it!

As I entered the jail that night, the first person to welcome me was the sergeant from the midnight shift. A Vietnam Army veteran, he immediately asked, "You must be the new guy?" He then added, "I heard you were in the Marines" and offered a strong handshake.

I responded, "Yes, Sergeant, that's correct." After a quick rundown of the essential rules, he guided me to the back area and introduced me to one of the senior officers.

My first night on the job was thrilling, even though there wasn't a lot going on with the inmates during that shift. It turned out to be the perfect opportunity for me to absorb everything around me. My partner, a fellow veteran who had served in the US Navy during Desert Storm, just like I did, provided great conversation throughout the night. Right away, I felt a sense of belonging; this was the connection I had been longing for. I truly missed the camaraderie of my fellow Marines.

Every shift presented its unique challenges. Thanks to the support of my fellow officers, I was able to adjust swiftly to my new role. I had the chance to work across all shifts and various stations within the jail facility. My responsibilities ranged from fingerprinting incoming inmates to managing difficult individuals. Occasionally, we even had the opportunity to join some of the deputies on patrol.

The moment arrived for the new officers to obtain their state certification. The county covered the costs, which meant we had to travel out of town for an entire week. A key component of the certification process involved taking a psychological assessment. I distinctly recall one question from the therapist: If I could be any two animals, which ones would I choose? My response was that I would opt to be an American bald eagle and a wild mustang. I truly admire the liberty that these two animals experience in their wild environment.

Once all the questions had been posed, we were instructed not to disclose or discuss our responses with anyone. Naturally, once we wrapped up and the officers gathered together, we began exchanging our answers. I remember some were quite amusing, while others left us pondering. The most hilarious response came from someone who said they wanted to be a frog and a rabbit—clearly, they had a fondness for jumping!

After the evaluations were completed, the therapist invited us in individually. When it was my turn, he inquired whether I intended to pursue a lifelong career in law enforcement. I affirmed that I did. His expression turned serious, and I found myself wondering what was coming next. He then declared, "You do not belong in law enforcement."

Confused, I responded, "Excuse me, sir, what do you mean by that?"

He then said, "Don't misunderstand me; I believe you'll excel in law enforcement, but I feel you're destined for something even greater." I was at a loss for words, unsure of how to reply. He continued, explaining that he didn't intend to dissuade me but rather wanted me to genuinely think about exploring a different career path. Naturally, I didn't heed his advice, but I think what he perceived that day was the divine calling God had on my life, one that I had been avoiding for quite some time.

After returning home, I sat down with my wife and had a long conversation about my career journey. I shared with her that, having gained a few months of experience in the sheriff's department, I was ready to begin applying to various city, state, and federal law enforcement agencies. To my surprise, she encouraged me to pursue what I believed was best for our future together.

With my wife's encouragement, I submitted applications to every agency and department imaginable. After about three to six months, the responses began to trickle in. Some letters expressed gratitude for my application but conveyed their regret in stating that there were no available positions at that moment. Others simply did not reply at all. After what felt like an eternity of waiting, I was thrilled to receive three job offers from different agencies: one from a major city police department, another from the state highway patrol, and the last from a federal law enforcement agency.

I went ahead and proceeded individually with each agency's hiring process. My plan was simple: I would go with the first one that offered me a position. During my interview with the police department, an older gentleman approached me and inquired about my name. After I introduced myself, he simply said, "Follow me."

Upon arriving at his office, he inquired if I recognized him, to which I replied, "No, sir." He then revealed that he was my uncle on my mother's side. He mentioned that he had learned about my applications, not just to his organization but also to a federal agency. He offered some advice, sharing that if he had the chance to start over, he would choose a federal path. While he left the decision to me, he strongly recommended pursuing the federal agency for better retirement and financial benefits.

My uncle, whom I had just met for the first time, kept sharing various pieces of advice about a career in law enforcement. One particular piece of advice that puzzled me back then was his suggestion to "leave work at work and home at home"—basically to keep work separate from my home life. Over the years, however, that advice has become increasingly clear and meaningful to me.

On numerous occasions the stress from work would spill over into my home life, impacting my mood and actions, and the same would happen in reverse. Managing this was quite a challenge. Eventually, the boundaries between my job and personal life began to bleed into one another. Truthfully, without some external support, it felt impossible to handle.

The long-awaited call finally arrived. I was in the shower, preparing for my evening shift at the jail, when my wife knocked on the door and shouted that a federal agency was on the line. I hurried out, shampoo still in my hair and a towel around me, to answer the phone. To my delight, it was a job offer, and I eagerly accepted it. I remember jumping up and down for joy after hanging up the phone. All I can say was I thank our Lord my in-laws weren't home at that moment.

I had anticipated that phone call for a duration of one year and ten months. When it finally arrived, it felt surreal. I had approximately one month remaining before commencing my training at the agency's academy. My wife and I were filled with joy, as we could finally perceive a glimmer of hope at the end of the tunnel.

During my time at the sheriff's office, which lasted around two years, I gained invaluable experience that I am truly grateful for. It provided me with a unique perspective on law enforcement that benefited me throughout my career. I forged some meaningful friendships during that period as well. Although I struggled with extreme hypervigilance, it proved to be an asset in the high-pressure atmosphere of the job. Interestingly, I discovered that this stressful environment had become my preferred norm.

The challenge arose when I returned home; without that familiar intensity, I often felt out of sync. While my relationship with my wife wasn't perfect, the daily responsibilities of life temporarily overshadowed the concerns about our marriage.

Traveling felt familiar again as I made my way to the Federal Law Enforcement Training Center, located in Georgia. Upon reaching my destination, I was greeted by a long white bus. Memories surged back, reminding me of a previous journey in another white bus, where I was greeted by a fierce group of Marine drill instructors, reminiscent of a pack of wolves. I felt a sense of calm and confidence this time. For some reason, I was convinced that whatever challenges lay ahead, the Lord had equipped me to face them.

I truly cherished my experience at the academy. I acquired numerous valuable skills that proved beneficial later. I also formed lasting friendships that have endured throughout my career. Although some days were challenging, particularly in my studies, the thrill of anticipating what lay ahead overshadowed any frustrations. Wearing that uniform for the first time made me feel right at home.

Graduation day had finally arrived, but my family couldn't make the long journey. However, when I landed at my hometown airport, this time I was greeted by my lovely bride, who was there waiting for me. I had so much to tell her, and things seemed to be looking up between us. I truly appreciated my wife's unwavering support throughout this journey.

I had roughly two weeks left before I needed to report to my first duty station. The bright side was that my assignment was in my home state of Texas, and I was taking my bride with me. We were both thrilled about the adventure ahead. My wife has always had a passion for travel, particularly when we could explore new places together. For her, this journey was particularly exhilarating.

I had made arrangements and rented a furnished one-bedroom apartment for us, making sure it was ready when we got there. Since we didn't have much back then, packing was a breeze. When we arrived at our new home, we realized it was the first time in a long while that we could live together for an extended period. While I was in the Marines, we had hardly spent more than two months together because of my frequent deployments. This was truly an exciting new beginning for us.

chapter three

HIGHWAY 44

*"There is a way that appears to be right, but in the end it
leads to death."*

PROVERBS 14:12

Everything was aligning perfectly, just as my wife and I had
envisioned. The chance to embark on my dream job was no
longer just a fantasy; it was now a tangible reality. I felt like
nothing could possibly derail this exciting journey. All my
hard work had finally borne fruit. Armed with fresh training
and renewed optimism, I was prepared to conquer whatever
came my way.

Unleashed Redemption
A K9 Handler's Story of Hope & Healing

On my inaugural day at work, I encountered a fascinating array of individuals. These folks were a unique mix, hailing from various places and boasting a wide range of experiences. I genuinely felt like I had found my place. The atmosphere reminded me of my time in the military, united by a common goal: national security.

My assigned supervisor greeted me with a firm handshake and introduced me to my fellow shift partners. We then participated in a shift muster, where we went over safety protocols and discussed our tasks for the day. After the meeting concluded, I was teamed up with a senior agent, and we were assigned our coverage area.

My new partner's opening line was, "Forget everything you learned at the academy!" I thought, *Oh boy, this is going to be interesting.* He quickly reassured me, saying, "Don't worry, I've got your back. I'll teach you everything you need to know to make it out here and get you home safely."

Each week, I was matched with a different individual. While everyone shared their unique insights, one older gentleman provided me with particularly valuable advice that continues to impact my life today. He said that everyone approaches things differently and has their own perspective to share. In time, you will cultivate your own style, but remember that everyone has something worthwhile to contribute; the trick is to embrace the positive and discard the negative.

I continue to follow this advice, and I agree that everyone has something valuable to offer. My experiences with both effective and ineffective leaders have taught me important lessons. Even from the less effective ones, I've gained insights into what not to do, which has ultimately shaped me into a more capable leader over time.

A year flew by in a flash, with each day presenting its own unique challenges—no two days were alike. We encountered a variety of tough and sometimes frustrating situations in the field, but the silver lining was that you were never on your own. A senior partner was always nearby who seemed to have an answer if you ever got into a jam, and the shift supervisor was just a radio call away as well. All in all, this job was incredibly fulfilling; as one of my partners put it, "It's hard to believe we actually get paid for this."

This career can be exciting or dull; it really hinges on the effort you put in and the decisions you make. Feeling stagnant is often a result of your own actions or lack thereof. The job offers various additional collateral duties, one of which was a canine handler role. After about two years in the field, an opportunity arose in one of these K9 roles: The station I worked at had a vacancy, but several more experienced agents had already applied for it. I decided not to submit my application, thinking that as a relatively new agent with only two years of experience, I wouldn't stand a chance.

To my astonishment, soon another canine handler position became available, but once more, I felt I lacked the seniority to apply. As I was about to leave at the end of a shift one day, a close friend with more experience approached me and asked if I had submitted my application for the role. I started to explain my hesitation when he took hold of my arm, guided me to a computer, and said, "Let me help you out with this."

The memorandum I submitted was the briefest I had ever composed, consisting of just three sentences. Nevertheless, that concise memo proved to be sufficient. Many of the senior agents who had previously expressed interest in the position chose to withdraw their memorandums, because they felt their chances were reduced when one of the top agents applied.

About a month passed, and I had accepted the idea that becoming a canine handler was not in my immediate future. Then, out of the blue, during an evening shift, my supervisor reached out to me, along with that friend who had encouraged me to apply for the canine role. A wave of anxiety washed over me as I wondered what we might have done wrong. I quickly began to review all the cases I had worked on, hoping I had meticulously attended to every detail.

To our surprise, the supervisor extended his hand toward us and offered his congratulations. We exchanged puzzled glances and simultaneously asked, "For what?" With a slight smirk, he replied, "You two are going to be the next canine handlers for this station. Pack your bags; you're set to leave in two days for a couple months at the National Canine Facility." We couldn't help but question him, "But how is this possible?" He clarified that the senior agent who had been selected previously had been bitten by his dog during training and, because of the bite, he chose to withdraw from the program, creating two openings at the station.

At that moment, all the senior agents were puzzled about why I had been chosen, considering I was still a junior agent. The supervisor quickly interjected, asking if they had submitted a memorandum for the position. The agents replied that they had withdrawn theirs since the role had already been filled by another senior agent. The supervisor then declared, "All right, I don't want to hear any more about it. Whether you're junior or not, I only had two memorandums on my desk."

On that day, I discovered an important lesson: never

underestimate yourself, especially without first giving it a shot. You never know what might unfold. Don't let negative voices sway you, especially when you've sought guidance through prayer and feel a sense of peace regarding your situation. I genuinely feel that day was divinely orchestrated, even though my commitment to God wasn't as strong then as it is now. It set off a series of events that ultimately led me to my current path.

DREAM REALIZED

After wrapping up our evening shift meeting, I hurriedly called my wife to share the exciting news. She was overjoyed, particularly because she found out that she could come and visit me at the training facility.

Two days flew by in a flash, and my friend and I were bursting with excitement. They handed my buddy a patrol car, as at that time the station was required to supply their own vehicles to the canine handlers. Meanwhile, I got stuck with a large, beat-up van. But honestly, I couldn't have cared less; I was too thrilled to worry about what kind of ride I had.

While heading to the training facility, I experienced a blowout on one of my rear tires. My friend and I were driving closely together, and he quickly pulled up behind me and turned on the red and blues. I was truly grateful for his support;

as I began to change the tire, I didn't anticipate him stepping in to help. To my surprise, he took the tire iron from me and said, "Let me give you a hand."

I worked alongside these kinds of guys every single day. They will genuinely give you the shirt off their back if you ever found yourself in a tough spot. The law enforcement community is like a close-knit family, much like the military or other first responders, where our lives truly rely on one another. Plus, the countless hours spent with your partners truly forge bonds that feel even stronger than family ties at times.

As I entered the classroom on the first day of canine handler training, I noticed that each student's desk was neatly arranged with a stack of books and training binders. Next to that were some office supplies and a personalized paper nameplate displaying each person's name.

This moment was incredibly thrilling for me. As I settled at my desk, memories of my middle school days flooded my mind. I distinctly recall dreaming of becoming a dog handler while observing the law enforcement officer and his Labrador retriever as they searched our lockers for any illegal items. Truly, I felt blessed.

A diverse group of law enforcement professionals from

across the nation were set to be my canine handler training classmates. This included individuals from various federal agencies, state troopers, and officers from local police departments. We were united as one team.

We spent roughly a week in the classroom, learning before we could even engage with the dogs. The curriculum included topics like canine behavior, safety protocols, handling techniques, first aid, and even canine case law. While the material was a bit demanding, anyone with a passion for dogs would have found this classroom experience enjoyable.

The long-awaited day finally arrived for us to begin our training with the dogs. That morning we were greeted by a new leather leash and a shiny fur saver dog collar resting on our desks. Before we ventured outside, we were given our kennel numbers and taught the proper way to attach the leash to our furry companions. Approaching the kennels, the atmosphere buzzed with anticipation, and the barking grew louder with each step we took.

As I neared my new partner, a Belgian Malinois named Rudie, he and the other dogs were barking loudly in a rather intimidating manner. I felt a bit reluctant to step into his kennel when, out of the blue, I heard a commanding voice behind me say, "Take your leash and collar and put it on that dog, now!"

After what felt like an eternity of struggling with the dog, I finally managed to secure the collar around his neck.

Once we placed the fur saver on our dogs, we were instructed to take them for a walk. The guidance was clear: no commands, just a leisurely stroll to bond with our furry companions. As I walked alongside my dog, I could see him glancing up at me, as if asking, "What can I do to make you happy, Dad?"

For about three days, we followed the same routine. When the instructors noticed that everyone was bonding with their dogs, they gave us the green light to bring our new partners home. It was an incredible experience as I loaded my dog and his belongings into the spacious van and headed to my room. Unloading him and bringing him inside was a moment like no other. From the start, Rudie and I hit it off. He was exceptionally obedient and loyal right from the beginning.

Each day began with more classroom instruction before we could dive into working with the dogs. The tasks involving the dogs were often tough and draining. By the end of each day, we returned to our hotel rooms feeling both mentally and physically exhausted. In those moments, I would recall my favorite drill instructor's tattoo that read: Pain is merely weakness leaving the body!

The training program spanned nearly two months, during which aspiring canine handlers had to excel not only in academic assessments but also in practical evaluations. Success depended on your ability to effectively manage and interpret your dog's behavior in real-world scenarios, as well as your dog reacting to your commands during search operations. Your overall performance in these two areas determined whether you would earn your certification or not.

The instructors provided our grades to us, one by one. When it was my turn and I got my score, the realization that I had passed filled me with joy—one of the happiest moments of my life. My aspiration to become a law enforcement canine handler had finally been realized.

Once we finished our training at the canine handler school, we took a moment to celebrate with our fellow handlers. We shared some laughs and some of our memorable stories with each other; it was a fun night. However, by the next morning, everyone had packed their bags, said their goodbyes, exchanged phone numbers, and started their journeys back home.

THE CROSSROADS

Upon arriving home, I introduced Rudie to my wife. Although she wasn't particularly a dog person, she soon grew to love

Rudie as if he were our own child. Before long, Rudie and I established a routine; the moment he spotted me in my uniform, he recognized it was time for fun. We adapted to the pace of work, and eventually, we even traded in that big old beat-up van and received our own patrol sedan.

My new position appeared to be going smoothly, and even my marriage felt like it was on the upswing. From the outside, everything looked flawless. I often found myself patrolling alone with my dog, which suited my introverted nature perfectly. However, I was unaware of the toll my solitary lifestyle was taking on me, as I missed the camaraderie with my colleagues that I had enjoyed before becoming a dog handler.

Eventually, I gave up on trying to fit in. The invitations to barbecues and birthday celebrations dwindled. Typically, when new employees joined, there would be a gathering within a month to celebrate the end of their probationary period. Since many of the newcomers didn't know me—having spent so much time alone in the field—I found myself left out. This only deepened my sense of isolation. I became intensely dedicated to my role as a canine handler, and my dog and I excelled in our work, earning several Top Dog awards. However, this success came at a cost.

The most challenging aspect was how this isolation began to impact my home life. I noticed I was turning to alcohol more during my free time. One of the deceptive thoughts that plagued me during that period, instigated by negativity, was the realization that my wife and I had been married for quite some time without being able to start a family. I couldn't shake the relentless voice in my head telling me that I would never become a father and would never experience the joys of parenthood.

In my third year as a dog handler, my drinking escalated. On my days off, I would either head straight to a bar or isolate myself at home with a drink in hand, trying to numb the sadness and anger that consumed me. Yet, amid the haze, a familiar voice echoed in my mind, reminding me, *This isn't who you are; this isn't the person I created you to be.* It was a voice I recognized from my childhood—God's voice—though I had been avoiding Him for quite some time. With each drink, that voice grew increasingly insistent.

One evening, while on my way to visit my father, I decided to stop by a bar. I realized it had started to rain, so I left early and was particularly cautious while driving. About halfway to my destination, a sheriff's deputy pulled me over. As he approached my car, he inquired about my driver's license and insurance. I told him I was heading to my dad's house nearby. He then asked if I had been drinking, and I admitted that I had. He requested that I step out of the vehicle and proceeded to administer a sobriety test. Once everything was finished, he informed me that I would be receiving a citation for reckless driving. Confused, I asked him why. He pointed out that I had missed a stop sign; my heart sank at his words.

A wave of deep regret washed over me. I realized that I had no one to blame but myself. I recalled reaching for a CD that had slipped to the floor, and it dawned on me that I must have overlooked the stop sign. The deputy could have easily charged me with driving under the influence. All the effort I had put into my career, all my hopes and dreams, felt like they were slipping away. Those thoughts consumed me as I made my way home.

I immediately reached out to my supervisor, who inquired whether I had been arrested or if my driver's license had been suspended. I clarified that I hadn't been arrested but had received a citation for reckless driving. He informed me that my manager would want to speak with me as soon as possible. When I showed up to work, my bosses were primarily focused on one issue: whether I still had my driver's license. I presented them with my citation and my license, and they reassured me that as long as I had my license and hadn't faced any arrest, everything was fine. They advised me to address that citation promptly.

For me, that was the breaking point; I felt like I had changed completely and was fed up with who I was. I continued to drink alcohol after that, but it just didn't feel the same anymore. God had been dealing with me strongly, especially after the incident.

As I strolled into the office one day, my eyes landed on a book resting atop the desk of one of my fellow canine handlers. The cover read *The God Chasers*, authored by Pastor Tommy Tenney. Curious, I inquired whether it was worth reading. My coworker assured me it was excellent and offered it to me since he had already completed it. Within about two weeks, I devoured the book, unable to put it down.

I had never really thought of myself as a "God chaser" until I read this book. It opened my eyes to a part of Christianity that I had only seen once before, through my grandmother's deep faith. Pastor Tenney emphasizes how the contrast between someone who is lukewarm and someone who is truly passionate for Christ can impact those around them. The important thing to remember is that it all begins with us;

God extends the invitation, but it's our choice to respond.

A few months later, while heading to work for my evening shift in my patrol car, I decided to pull over on the side of Highway 44 and turned on my hazard lights. In that moment, I completely surrendered everything to God. I remember saying to Him, "God, I know you're real, and I'm tired. I'm not entirely sure what this Christianity stuff is all about, but if you can use this mess, here I am!"

I didn't witness any fireworks or hear a choir of angels singing, but at that instant, a profound peace washed over me, unlike anything I had ever experienced before. I felt a big weight lift off my shoulders and found myself crying uncontrollably, but it was a joyful cry. I even think my service dog was born again along with me on that day. I could hear him licking the partition behind me and yelping as if he were trying to comfort me.

I was so excited to get home after work that day, eager to share the wonderful news with my wife. However, when I finally told her what was on my mind, I was taken aback by her reaction. After I explained that I had committed my life to God and planned to live for Him from now on, she looked at me as if I had lost my mind.

She expressed her belief that it wouldn't work out and

suggested that perhaps we should consider a divorce. Her reasoning was that if we had both been struggling in our marriage as "devils," then with me trying to be a "saint" and her remaining as she was, there was no way we could make it work.

I shared with her that she was free to make her own choices, but I wanted her to know how much I truly cared for her and that I was committed to making our relationship work. However, I also expressed that I had decided to prioritize God in my life moving forward.

I emphasized that my faith was a personal journey and that I would never pressure her into anything she wasn't comfortable with. This lesson came from my grandmother, who taught me that faith is a personal choice; God invites us into a relationship with Him out of love, never through force.

WILLING TO LAY IT ALL DOWN

I recall going to church alone quite often, which felt a bit isolating, but I found a sense of peace knowing that everything would turn out all right. I asked the Lord how I could encourage my wife to join me at church. Should I compel her, place handcuffs on her, or pull her along? Then, I heard Him say: *All I want you to do is love her, no matter what.* I questioned, *No matter what, Lord?* And He affirmed, *No matter what!*

It took about three months for her to see a genuine change in me. I recall my wife questioning how one could love someone they couldn't see, and how did one love God? I suggested she ask Him to reveal how to love Him, and He would. She then expressed that she wanted to experience what I had and asked if she could join me at church the next time I went.

Waiting for my wife to accompany me to church felt like an eternity. Throughout that time, I kept my faith strong, praying for God to reach her heart without ever pressuring her. However, while I waited, I prayed over and anointed with oil each piece of clothing and every item she possessed. I also remember dedicating our home to God, holding onto the promise of Joshua 24:15, which says, "But as for me and my household, we will serve the LORD."

My wife finished her work one evening and was astonished to realize she had declined an invitation to a party thrown by her colleagues. Both she and her friends were shocked by her decision. When she returned home, she was filled with excitement and eager to share the wonderful news with me. She repeatedly exclaimed, "I said no, and I truly meant it." For her, this was a true sign that God was beginning to work in her life, especially since she had accepted Jesus as her Lord just two weeks earlier.

We began going to church consistently, and I recall how deeply I immersed myself in the Word of God. I dedicated countless hours to studying His Word. My wife also prioritized our time in prayer together, which strengthened our bond. We had numerous questions, and just when we needed guidance, God sent us a mentor. This wonderful man, simply known as Brother Joe, a retired schoolteacher and Bible instructor, was always sharing the message of Jesus with anyone he encountered.

We first met this man at our former church, where he was assisting our pastor with various teachings. After a Sunday service, we went out for lunch together, and to our surprise, my wife discovered that she had met him before. She used to work as a cashier at a nearby grocery store, and he had stopped by her register one day to ask if she knew Jesus. This man has truly been a wonderful blessing in our lives.

At work, I noticed a shift in my feelings. While I still cherished my role as a canine handler and enjoyed my job, my focus had begun to change. I felt a deep desire to fulfill God's purpose for me, but I was uncertain about the path to take. One evening, while I was alone at home and my wife was at work,

I found myself in prayer. I placed my badge and gun on the bed and said, "Lord, if you want me to pursue full-time ministry, I'm willing to let this go for you." In that moment, I heard a clear response: *You are my son whom I have called to be a law enforcement officer; you are not merely a law enforcement officer who I have called to be my son.*

I felt a profound clarity about the message from my heavenly Father. He had chosen me to be among law enforcement officers, to connect as one who truly understood their experiences. I realized that my calling was to serve as a minister to the law enforcement community. As I shared my thoughts with a colleague about possibly stepping away from the badge and gun, he unknowingly affirmed my purpose. He looked at me and said, "Why would you do that? Just look around; this is your congregation!"

Not long after, on the crisp morning of September 11, 2001, I recall having breakfast with a few colleagues. While we were enjoying our meal, a special news broadcast appeared on the television. It displayed shocking footage of planes crashing into the Twin Towers of the World Trade Center in New York, along with heartbreaking scenes of people leaping from the buildings due to the raging fires.

We were immediately placed on high alert, and by that

evening, many of us found ourselves boarding government-owned planes, the only flights allowed at that moment. We were dispatched to different international airports as part of security protocols. We had no idea where we were headed until we arrived; all we were instructed to do was pack for a trip that would last a couple weeks.

I ending up being gone a few months rather than weeks, but finally, it was time to return home. Our country had transformed; for a fleeting moment, everyone had come together. We were a nation in mourning, and we craved connection. Places of worship overflowed with people; the colors of red, white, and blue adorned every corner; and kindness flowed freely among us.

I had the opportunity to share my faith with several law enforcement officers from different agencies during my assignment. While some embraced the message and others did not, I felt grateful to convey a message of hope, especially when hope seemed to be in short supply.

A NEW VISION

My journey with K9 Rudie felt like it was reaching its conclusion. After five years as a canine handler, the opportunity for promotion was fast approaching. To be considered for advancement, my overall score would be based on a combination of collateral duties, assignments, and experience. If I wanted the chance to have my name in the running, I needed to tackle a few more collateral tasks.

Rudie and I had been members of the Special Response Team (SRT), which helped me maintain a solid level of fitness throughout that period. I made the decision to become a certified physical training instructor. Once I earned my certification, I received an invitation to teach at the Federal Law Enforcement Training Center, located in South Carolina, for the next set of classes. I felt ready in every aspect—physically, mentally, and spiritually.

The wonderful news was that my wife could join me while I was at the academy as an instructor. We had a fantastic time during our stay. As soon as we arrived at our temporary home, our first priority was to locate a church to attend. While at the academy, I made some great friends who really helped us feel comfortable and at home.

Six months passed quickly, and when we returned, I felt passionate to embrace the world for Jesus. As I explored additional responsibilities, a chance arose: I was invited to serve as a chaplain in my sector. At that time, the chaplaincy program wasn't yet a national initiative. The only stipulation was that I needed to be an ordained minister from an external organization. Having recently become ordained, I eagerly accepted the opportunity.

My wife and I began to pray with devotion, and as we sought God more earnestly, we discovered numerous opportunities to serve Him. We started volunteering at our church, driven by a strong desire to help others. We supported our former pastor in various tasks that the church required. Being part of a small country church meant many opportunities to get involved. I took on roles ranging from managing media to ushering, and over time, the pastor entrusted me with greater responsibilities, eventually appointing me as a deacon and later as a minister.

The pastor eventually approached my wife and me with a request to help in the children's ministry and even take on the youth program. We were truly touched and agreed to take on the roles. I recall my wife and I wondering how we could do this since we didn't have any children of our own. I felt like God was preparing us for something bigger. We dedicated ourselves wholeheartedly to the children's ministry, treating and loving every child as if they were part of our family. I even picked up a few cowboy chords to play songs for them on my acoustic guitar.

Everything seemed to be falling into place. At work, I was

dedicated to serving the Lord through the chaplaincy program, embracing every opportunity that arose. I was even invited to help with funerals and memorial services for various agencies and local organizations. For the first time, I truly sensed that I was making a meaningful impact.

But still an emptiness lingered in my heart that my wife and I had been bringing to God in our prayers. We had made the decision to adopt after numerous visits to the doctor, who advised us not to pursue having a child. We kept praying, asking God to grant us peace if it was His plan for us to adopt. Conversely, if adoption wasn't in His plans for us, we sought the comfort to wait and trust on His timing. Years passed, and we found ourselves at peace with the decision to wait rather than adopt.

We wholeheartedly dedicated ourselves to the children's ministry, pouring our energy and passion into every moment. Eventually, the pastor invited me to teach Sunday school for the adults, and I eagerly embraced the opportunity. This experience significantly deepened my faith, as it required me to immerse myself more in the Word of God with devotion and commitment.

One night, I experienced a profound dream that lingered with me long after I woke up. In this dream, I found myself walking through a vast desert, accompanied by two towering figures on either side of me. Suddenly, I spotted a rattlesnake blocking my path, and I distinctly heard the voice of the Lord urging me to pick it up and throw it as far as I could. Without hesitation, I obeyed and tossed it away, feeling no fear in that moment.

After that, I sprinted toward a river where I saw an oak tree with a treehouse nestled in its branches. Inside the treehouse was my wife, who was pregnant. The tree appeared to be collapsing, so I rushed to rescue her. I vividly remember getting her out just in time, unharmed. Later, God revealed the significance of this dream, showing that any curse that had been upon my wife and me had been lifted by the blood of Christ.

One Saturday afternoon, my wife and I were engaged in prayer at home when suddenly, I was immersed in the presence of the Lord. His voice was unmistakable, asking me about the deepest desire of my heart. With certainty, I replied, "Lord, I want to share your Word with the world!" But then He gently pressed further, *Son, you know what I'm truly asking. What is your heart's true desire?* As I began to answer, the Lord, already aware of my innermost thoughts, proclaimed, *By this time tomorrow, you will have a baby boy, and you shall name him Jedidiah.*

I had never even heard of the name Jedidiah before, so I initially thought I had simply overlooked it in the Bible, which means *beloved of the Lord.* The moment those words registered, an overwhelming wave of emotion hit me, and I began to cry like never before. I shared this revelation with my wife, and as soon as I did, she burst into tears as well. We were unable to contain our emotions.

My wife later shared with me something that I was unaware of. She had been diligently praying to the Lord, recalling the stories of every barren woman mentioned in the Bible. During her prayer sessions, she spoke with God, expressing her belief that He does not show favoritism. She was confident that if He had blessed the women in the Bible, He could bless us too. With a heart full of faith, she asked the Lord for just a word, promising that she would embrace it.

My incredible experience occurred on December 28. By January 12, I returned home and discovered a pregnancy test displaying a positive result on the bathroom counter. It was one of the happiest days of my life! Later, I learned from my Bible studies that when God says, "by this time tomorrow," it signifies a year's time. True to the Word of God, my son arrived the following September.

Unleashed Redemption
A K9 Handler's Story of Hope & Healing

When asked why I choose to serve the Lord, my answer is simple: How could I possibly do otherwise? Since we've committed our lives to Him, the journey has not been without its difficulties. We have faced numerous challenges, yet we continue to move forward in faith.

chapter four

HE WILL USE OUR BATTLES

"The LORD who rescued me from the paw of the lion and the paw of the bear will rescue me from the hand of this Philistine."

1 SAMUEL 17:37

Victory often comes with its share of struggles. After I returned to work following the birth of my child at a place a significant distance from my hometown, I was greeted with some disheartening news. The agency had chosen to upgrade everyone's General Schedule (GS) pay grade level, which eliminated my opportunity to transfer to a station nearer to my hometown. Prior to this, I had been offered a position at a station closer to home, but with these new changes, all transfers to different stations were abruptly canceled.

Additionally, the promotion process had been revamped. Instead of advancing based on points accumulated through experience and assignments, promotions were now determined solely by scores on an assessment test. This change meant I would essentially have to start from scratch.

I found myself caught in a transition between the old ways and the new. Many of my senior colleagues had already been promoted, while younger agents were advancing based on their test scores. I felt trapped in a cycle with no way out.

I realized I had two options: I could wallow in my sadness and pity myself, or I could place my trust in God and move ahead, regardless of what lay in front of me or what I had yet to see. I made the choice to place my trust in God, turning to Him in prayer to seek peace regarding my circumstances.

I recalled the comforting words from Jeremiah 29:11: "'For I know the plans I have for you,' says the Lord, 'plans to prosper you and not to harm you, plans to give you hope and a future.'" I remember expressing to Him, "Lord I don't understand what you're doing in my life, but I trust you and I will be obedient to you."

TRUST

Following the events of 9/11, the agency underwent significant transformations, with one of the most notable being the shift toward national initiatives for many of its programs. What had previously been managed at a local level was now standardized across the country. The chaplaincy program was elevated to a national initiative, similar to other programs, requiring all chaplains to complete a screening process and attend a Chaplaincy Academy. During this transition, a new initiative, the Peer Support Program, was established, enabling agents to provide support to their colleagues and their families in times of need.

Management recognized that I was waiting for a Chaplaincy Academy date and contacted me to see if I could take part in the Peer Support Program training in the interim, representing the station. Upper management was looking for people to attend and help make this initiative successful. I was more than happy to take part; I felt God was up to something new, and I was eager to respond to that call.

During my time at the training, I found myself deeply engaged. The trainers delved into essential subjects such as suicide prevention and intervention, grief support, stress management, and other relevant themes. As a minister and chaplain, I had encountered these issues before, but this training offered a more in-depth exploration. I was reminded of a message I had received from my Lord some time ago: "I have called you to be one of them."

As a chaplain, I often saw that only people with a religious background felt at ease coming to me. When I tried to connect with those who didn't have that background, many appeared unsure and hesitant to talk to me. I also noticed this hesitation when I was a peer support member; when I reached out to someone in need, they sometimes seemed unsure at first. However, by not pressuring anyone and showing that I had no hidden agenda, they gradually began to trust me as they realized I was there to help. In this new role, I was able to connect with people I usually wouldn't have reached.

A quote from my pastor really speaks to me and matches my experience in the Peer Support Program: "People will not care until they know you care." This program has been a true blessing in my life. During my journey with the Lord, I've learned that He often works in surprising ways. When you allow the Spirit of God to guide you, even if things don't go as planned, He can take just two small fish and five loaves of bread and turn them into something amazing that you never expected.

Serving as a chaplain was truly one of the highlights of my law enforcement journey, and I cherished every experience. Eventually, I faced the difficult choice of which program to commit to. I determined that it would be more advantageous to focus on just one resiliency program rather than juggling two. After much reflection and prayer, I felt a strong call to continue my work with the Peer Support Program.

IT IS NOT ABOUT US

In this chapter of my life, I discovered numerous insights, but one lesson shines the brightest. The most significant realization I had was the importance of prioritizing others over myself. I learned that when I surrender my struggles to God, He will fight my battles for me. His power can achieve more in a single moment than we can in an entire lifetime. I found that by genuinely focusing on the needs of others, even during my own difficult times, He consistently provided for me in various ways.

A few years had gone by since the birth of my first son, and to our astonishment, another miracle was on its way. We had noticed my wife feeling unusually fatigued, but we couldn't pinpoint the reason. One day, as she lay in bed looking worn out, I playfully remarked, "You must be pregnant." We both laughed it off, thinking it was just a joke. However, as her fatigue continued to worsen, I persuaded her to visit the doctor for a check-up. To our surprise, when she returned home, she shared the wonderful news: "Congratulations, you're going to be a daddy again!"

I recall a moment when I thought, *Oh my goodness, you've done it once more, Lord. How can I ever repay you?* The doctors had previously told us that having children might not be in our future, especially before our first child arrived. But for God, nothing is impossible. We are not more special than anyone else; we face our own challenges too. However, I truly believe that what makes all the difference is our unwavering pursuit of Him, regardless of the obstacles we encounter.

Just when I believed I had seen it all, God surprised me yet again with the extraordinary. When I surrendered my heart and expressed my willingness for Him to use my life, I never anticipated the incredible ways He would move in my journey.

My wife and I began hosting Bible studies in our home, feeling a divine calling to share God's Word with our neighbors, friends, and family. What initially started as casual gatherings with just a couple of friends over coffee quickly blossomed into a vibrant mini service. It was astonishing to see how eager people were to receive the Word of God, and we found ourselves like bakers offering warm, fresh bread straight from the Father.

We opened our home and our hearts to everyone, and we experienced God moving in an extraordinary way unlike anything we had encountered before. Those who were unfamiliar with the Lord came and found hope; demons were expelled, and many were set free and healed. We saw the Scriptures come to life in a miraculous manner, all because we chose to be obedient and faithful to His calling.

One Sunday afternoon, our Bible teaching mentor reached out to me, asking if we could talk. He shared that God had put it on his heart to invite me to pastor a small nondenominational church. Little did Brother Joe know, he was affirming the very calling that God had already begun to stir within me.

Making the shift from being a minister to pastoring at the church was relatively smooth, as many of the attendees were familiar faces from our home Bible studies. I served as a pastor on a volunteer basis, without any salary. The real challenge came from balancing my full-time job and shift work alongside my pastoral duties. Nevertheless, I remained committed to the calling God had placed on my heart.

In that church, I witnessed the powerful presence of God; although we were a small group, we served an immense God. My experience as a pastor taught me invaluable lessons. I realized that being a pastor differs significantly from being a minister; it requires a deep commitment to spiritually support those entrusted to your care, acting as a vigilant guardian for them. The bonds I formed with those individuals grew to be as strong as those with my own family. I felt their pain, their joy, and every heartache they faced.

Being a pastor profoundly shaped my approach even with my colleagues, supervisors, and managers at work, revealing insights I had previously overlooked. I realized that my purpose wasn't limited to helping just a few individuals; rather, I was meant to be a source of support for everyone around me. As a peer support member, I found that God used this role to cultivate a sense of compassion within me that I had never experienced before. In my past, before embracing my faith, my focus was solely on myself. I remember the deep sense of isolation I felt after my time in the military, and how my anger, fueled by selfishness, consumed me.

My wife and I remained dedicated to our ministry, following wherever God led us. He provided opportunities for me to serve not only at our church but also at various nearby congregations. Our passion for service was strong, and we managed to balance this commitment with my shift work. I am grateful for my job, as it allowed the church's offerings to be directed solely toward covering utilities and supporting international outreach efforts in places like Israel, Africa, and beyond.

I would have never imagined in a million years that God would choose to work through me as He has and continues to do so even now. Being an introvert and quite shy by nature, it's surprising to see how things have unfolded. It's almost as if God has a playful sense of humor! I often joke with the congregation, saying that if He can make a mute man speak, then I've certainly been given a voice that won't quit. I remind them that this transformation must be divine, as I've never been one to enjoy talking. As a child, coaxing even two words out of me was quite an achievement. The Lord was simply saving all those words for my journey as a preacher.

There's a fire ignited within me that I simply cannot hold back. I feel compelled to share it with the world, and with each act of sharing, it only grows stronger. God has instilled in me a deep compassion for those who are lost and suffering, to the point where my own selfish desires have diminished, and my yearning to fulfill His purpose has intensified.

As I've mentioned before, engaging in ministry often invites challenges, and sometimes the most painful wounds come from those closest to us. This has taught me an important truth: Our struggles are not merely against physical circumstances; the opposition we encounter is of a spiritual nature, which means that only God can truly fight our battles. Our role is to place our trust in Him and find our peace in His presence.

A NEW TEAM

One afternoon, my supervisor came to me and mentioned that management was looking to expand the number of canine handlers. They were specifically interested in agents who had previous experience, as the only requirement would be to recertify with a new dog. I inquired about how quickly he needed a response, and he told me I had until the next day. That evening, I returned home and asked my wife if she would join me in prayer to discern whether it was God's will for me to become a canine handler once more.

We received the peace to move forward with the new role as a dog handler. At the same time, I was still actively involved in pastoring and heavily engaged with the Peer Support Program. By this stage, I had also joined the Critical Incident Response Team as a peer support member. Our goal was to assist agents deployed on rescue and support missions following natural disasters or critical incidents.

As I headed back to the National Canine Training Facility,

memories of my beloved K9, Rudie, flooded my mind. After serving faithfully, Rudie was retired at the age of eleven, and since I had been his first handler and spent the most time with him, they offered him to me. I was thrilled to take him in, and he enjoyed a joyful retirement until he passed away at fourteen.

My family quickly grew to adore him, treating him as one of our own. K9 Rudie was truly a blessing in my life, holding a unique place in my heart, especially as he stood by me through both my darkest moments and my greatest triumphs.

For a long time, he was the sole confidant of my deepest struggles. I recall those long hours we spent patrolling the highways, keeping an eye on traffic. During those moments, I would open up to him about my innermost thoughts. I understood that my K9 couldn't grasp my words, but it felt like a healthy release for me. This was back in the days before smartphones and social media took over. It was simply a classic sit-and-wait situation, one that I came to cherish and value.

I deeply cherish the memories I created with K9 Rudie, and as I reflect on those moments, I am genuinely grateful to my Lord for them. In terms of operations, Rudie was the finest partner any handler could wish for. His obedience was unmatched, he exuded confidence, worked seamlessly with the team, adored people, and had an incredible sense of smell. He will always hold a special place in my heart.

Stepping into the classroom, the sight of the towering stacks of books and binders instantly transported me back to my initial experience at the K9 Academy. This time, my stay would be shorter since I only needed to certify with my dog. Nevertheless, I was thrilled to return; the familiar atmosphere was comforting. The instructors paired me with a group of handlers who were nearing the completion of their training.

I was given a dog named Bunker, a brindle-colored Dutch shepherd. He was slightly larger than Rudie and not quite as sociable. As I began my work with him, I was grateful for my previous experience as a handler. Still, I realized that K9 Rudie had set a high standard with his obedience. I quickly realized that every dog has its own unique personality.

K9 Bunker was what you might call an alpha dog, and he didn't hesitate to test me from the very start. I knew I had to establish my position as the alpha, not him. It took some time, but by diligently applying the guidance from my trainers, I managed to conquer this challenge and break down that barrier.

In K9 training, one of the first lessons we learned as handlers was that it's not a matter of if you'll get bitten, but when. Sure enough, just a few days into working with my new partner, we wrapped up a training exercise, and as I reached to grab a reward object from my dog, it happened.

I vividly recall the instructor glancing at me and asking, "Did that dog just bite you?" I responded, "Yes, sir, he did." The instructor seemed taken aback and asked why I hadn't mentioned it. I suppose he was surprised that I didn't even flinch and continued working despite the blood trickling down my arm. With a hint of frustration, he instructed me to put the dog away and head to the medic to get the bite checked out.

Throughout my years with K9 Rudie, he never once even growled at me—not even a hint of aggression. He was the kind of dog who would let me take his food bowl while he was eating without a second thought. But then there was Bunker; I quickly realized I was in for quite a wild ride. This dog had a strong will, and not in the best way. Since it took several attempts to get him engaged in a search, I had to make some adjustments to my approach to bring him up to a working level.

The time to get certified with him arrived sooner than expected. Although we weren't the best match as a team, I managed to adapt. The day after our certification, I began my journey home with my new dog. Bunker and I didn't share the same bond that I had with Rudie. As soon as I introduced the new K9 to my family, I cautioned them that he was different from Rudie and advised them to keep their distance. Unsurprisingly, my family never connected with Bunker in the same way they had with Rudie.

My family and I recognized that he wasn't a pet; he was a working dog, and we respected that role. Over time, I began to bond with Bunker, although our connection was quite different from the one I had with Rudie.

HE TRAINS OUR HANDS FOR WAR

Changes at work had become a constant since 9/11, with an influx of new policies and restrictions imposed by Washington, DC. These measures often hindered our field operations. Yet, as resilient agents, we adapted and found ways to make it all work.

As an agency, we faced increasing challenges with every new administration and the frequent shifts in upper management. We learned to navigate these changes, some of which proved beneficial, while others, not so much. Nevertheless, we remained focused on our primary goal: ensuring national security.

Considering that, Bunker and I got down to business. One thing was clear: this new dog was relentless; he simply wouldn't back down. His strong personality meant I needed to find a way to effectively redirect that energy. I sensed that God was guiding me through a lesson I couldn't yet understand, but I had to believe that it would ultimately lead to something good.

A year later, it happened again: My service dog and I were on a call when he suddenly emerged with something white in his mouth. My heart sank as I rushed to take it from him, and in the process, he bit my hand for the second time. I realized it was my mistake for not following our training protocol. Thankfully, the object turned out to be just an apple he had grabbed, rather than something harmful.

My time with Bunker was filled with challenges that ultimately became valuable lessons. I was unaware at the time, but these experiences would benefit me down the road. Throughout it all, I maintained my faith in the Lord. I not only served as a dog handler for several years but continued with the roles as a peer support member and pastor. At times, the frustrations of working with a service dog would seep into my home life and even affect my interactions with my church community.

I reached a point where I needed to reassess whether my actions were truly serving a purpose. I realized that my experience serving with Bunker had turned into a weight I was carrying. I no longer found joy in my role as a handler, and even though I was performing my duties to the best of my ability, my passion had faded. I realized it was time to move forward. This is a lesson I had learned much earlier in life: When I engage in activities for the Lord, if they start to feel like a burden, then they're not being a blessing to anyone.

chapter five

GIVING UP THE LEASH

"The Lord makes firm the steps of the one who delights in him; though he may stumble, he will not fall, for the Lord upholds him with his hand."

PSALM 37:23–24

One of the toughest choices I've ever faced was letting go of the leash. It wasn't an easy call to make, but it was essential. I realized that this marked the conclusion of my canine handler career. When I finally stepped down from that role, I felt like I was grieving, yet deep down, I understood it was the right thing to do. Being a canine handler comes with its advantages, but if you aspire to advance in rank, it's essential to prepare yourself and adopt a mindset of responsibility as a supervisor. I realized that staying in the role of a canine handler would mean missing out on another chance for promotion.

I had passed the assessment test and achieved a solid score, sufficient to begin applying for supervisor positions at different locations. After discussing it with my wife, we both realized how much we had come to appreciate our current area, so we decided that I would apply to supervisor positions that were conveniently located nearby.

I focused on collateral responsibilities that would enhance my skills as a supervisor. This involved volunteering as an acting supervisor and refreshing my knowledge of field operations in my role as a regular agent. I strongly felt that God was directing me in a new direction once again.

I submitted applications to three nearby locations, but I felt God was drawing me to a fourth one, even though I hesitated to apply there. After multiple attempts with the other three options, I continued to be overlooked. After much prayer, I finally felt compelled to apply at that fourth location. To my surprise, as soon as I did, I received a call from management offering me a position there.

This opportunity to be a supervisor was clearly a divine appointment. I was reminded of Jonah, who initially resisted God's call to Nineveh. It took a massive fish to change his mind and lead him to his destined path. God has a way of being gentle, but I've come to realize that if we continue to disregard His guidance, He has a unique ability to capture our focus. When I finally listened, through prayer, and understood where He wanted me to be, I followed His lead, and what I discovered there was truly remarkable.

I remember asking the manager who called me how quickly he needed my response regarding the job offer. I couldn't help but think that he might have wondered if I had lost my mind by asking how much time I had. Opportunities to become a supervisor are rare, and typically, people seize them right away. He could have easily said, "If you're not interested, I'll just move on to the next person," but thankfully, he told me I had until the end of the day to decide.

My response highlights how immature I was at that time—what was I even thinking? A friend of mine, who managed a different location where I had applied, called me a few days prior to let me know I had made the final list for that area.

I reached out to him for some guidance and brought up the job offer I received from the other location. I can still hear him raising his voice, urging me to accept it! He emphasized that just being on the list doesn't ensure anything; a lot can change before the final decisions are made.

After a bit of hesitation on my part, I finally decided to call the manager back and accept the supervisor position. He congratulated me and provided me with the date I would start at the new station. I felt a surge of excitement about what opportunities awaited me there. After years of prayer, this moment had finally arrived, and it came when I least expected it. I had been so focused on being faithful in my current role that I had nearly given up on my aspirations for advancement. Once, this had been one of my greatest desires, and while I had prayed for it, it had shifted to a lower priority in my life.

I had come to terms with the idea that if my God wanted me to serve as a senior agent for the entirety of my career, I would embrace that role with unwavering dedication. Yet, I couldn't help but feel a deep sense of gratitude for the new path God was unfolding before me.

Psalm 37:4 reminds us, "Take delight in the LORD, and he will give you the desires of your heart." This isn't merely a promise of prosperity or a magical wish-granting scenario; it goes much deeper than that. It invites us into a meaningful relationship with God, much like the way a devoted parent cares for their child.

When we learn to find joy in Him, our focus shifts, and the fleeting vain desires that once occupied our hearts begin to diminish. The beauty of this transformation is that as we prioritize Him, He begins to entrust us with the blessings He's had in store for us so we will glorify Him and be a blessing to others.

MY NINEVEH

On the day I arrived at my new station, I unexpectedly found myself locked outside the gates. Access required either a code or a scan card. Fortunately, I've always made it a habit to arrive early for any appointment or event, a practice I attribute to my military background. Just as I was about to call the station for assistance, a supervisor pulled up in a sleek black Trans Am. I approached him and introduced myself as one of the new supervisors, but the look he gave me was so intense that I felt as if I might not survive the encounter.

This gentleman didn't say much more than a simple, "Follow me." I really didn't want to ask, but as soon as we parked in the back, he guided me through the rear entrance of the building. He pointed me in the right direction and mentioned a specific manager to ask for. I couldn't help but think, *Wow, if this is how the welcoming committee operates,*

Unleashed Redemption
A K9 Handler's Story of Hope & Healing

I wonder what the rest of the group will be like. I thought, *Here we go, in the name of Jesus.*

I entered the manager's office and introduced myself, noticing that another newly hired supervisor was already there. He was an agent who had been promoted from within, and today was his first day in this role, just like mine. I learned that the manager had begun his career at this very station and had stayed there ever since. He was a friendly and upbeat gentleman, nothing like the last fellow I had just met.

The manager quickly made us feel at ease and asked us to hang around until the other newly hired supervisors arrived. Once everyone was present, we were all invited into the muster area. In comparison to my previous station, this muster room was nearly as large as the entire building of my last workplace.

As we began to introduce ourselves, I realized that this group of newly appointed supervisors hailed from various corners of the country. Each individual contributed a unique background and a wealth of experience to the gathering.

The agent in charge of the station stepped forward to introduce himself and extend a warm welcome to everyone. He provided us with a brief overview of their operations, shared some intelligence insights, and outlined their key priorities. Following that, we enjoyed a guided tour of the station, where we were assigned to our respective offices and office partners. The supervisors shared a common office space, while the managers had their own separate areas.

Overall, it turned out to be a solid first day. We spent the entire week on day shift, familiarizing ourselves with the station's layout before being assigned to our individual units. Once we settled into our respective areas, most of the supervisors were supportive individuals who understood that each person's success as an individual was tied to each other. However, a few took a different approach, believing that if they had to navigate challenges alone, so should we.

As the dust settled, I found myself pondering, *Lord, what is your purpose for bringing me here?* Before long, He started to reveal the deep spiritual needs surrounding me. I noticed many disheartened and wounded employees yearning for a way out of their despair. Their faces mirrored the anguish I once felt. I held the answer, but the challenge was in how to share it. I placed my trust in the Lord, confident that He would unveil an opportunity in due time.

During our orientation as new supervisors, management requested that we complete a form detailing our personal information. One of the questions inquired about any certifications or unique skill sets we held. I listed my qualifications, which included peer support, chaplaincy, K9 handler, prosecutions, and various other collateral duties and certifications I had acquired along the way.

A manager who played a significant role in the Peer Support Program came up to me and inquired whether my certification as a peer support member was current. I happily confirmed, "Yes, sir, it is." He replied positively, saying that my skills would be a great asset there. Then, he asked about my chaplaincy status. I explained that I hadn't participated in the chaplaincy program since it had become a national program, but that I was an ordained minister and pastor through another organization. His response was simply, "Good, good!"

I quickly dove into the task at hand. The great part was that the work I encountered here closely resembled what I had tackled at my previous station, only this time on a larger scale. Despite the increased workload, it surprisingly felt lighter, thanks to the many hands available to assist throughout the process.

My new work environment contrasted greatly with that at my prior station. I had attempted to discuss the poor working conditions with management there, but unfortunately my concerns went nowhere. At my last post, one morning, after finishing a midnight shift, I had approached the agent in charge and asked if I could have a quick word with him. I felt at ease doing this because he had previously served as my special response team commander.

He welcomed me into his office. I expressed my concern about the rising number of arrests and traffic, which had led agents to work double and even triple shifts. I pointed out that this intense schedule had resulted in a few incidents where agents' vehicles veered off the road and one had even rolled over because they had dozed off on their way home. Additionally, I highlighted that many agents were facing marital issues, as they were rarely at home, and even divorce.

With a look of frustration, he asked, "What do you want me to do?" He mentioned that his hands were tied but he would reach out to the union about it. He seemed to think I was representing the union, so I took a moment to clarify that I was just a peer support member, there to express my concerns about the well-being of the agents.

The assistant agent in charge then entered the room and inquired about my recommendations for resolving the issue. I suggested that they could relay any information that wasn't relevant to the case to the next shift, rather than burdening the entire team, particularly after a late-night shift. Again, I wasn't yet a supervisor at that time; I was simply a senior agent. Nevertheless, I've always had a strong desire to advocate for those who may not be able to speak up in situations where fairness is at stake.

My goal was never to show disrespect; I simply wanted to highlight the importance of the agents' well-being and that of their families. Yet, the reply I received from the assistant agent in charge was quite dismissive. He stated, "I've been at this for years, and I bleed green [the color of our uniform]! I've handled countless cases without ever voicing a complaint about the workload."

Realizing I wasn't going to make any progress with them, I calmly stated, "Sir, with all due respect, I'm not here to complain. This isn't even about me; I'm a dog handler, and my position comes with a cap on hours that prevents me from working extra. My supervisors send me home automatically. I'm here solely to draw attention to the welfare of the agents and their families."

The man responded with a simple, "Okay, thank you."

HOPE IN DARKNESS

As I committed myself to my role as a supervisor at my new station, I made a conscious effort to immerse myself in the daily operations and challenges faced by the agents. I understood that my position was not just about overseeing tasks and ensuring compliance; it was about fostering a supportive environment where each agent felt valued and heard. I took the time to learn about their individual strengths, aspirations, and concerns, demonstrating that I was genuinely invested in their well-being rather than merely fulfilling a duty.

In the beginning, the agents were understandably cautious. They had seen supervisors come and go, some more interested in maintaining authority than in building relationships. However, as I consistently made myself available and approachable, they began to see a different side of leadership. I encouraged open dialogue, inviting them to share their thoughts and ideas, and I actively listened to their feedback.

Over time, they started to visit my office more frequently, eager to engage in conversations that went beyond the usual work-related topics. They shared their successes, sought advice on challenges, and even discussed personal matters, which deepened our connection. Slowly but surely, I built their trust. I made it a point to follow through on my promises, whether it was advocating for their needs in meetings or providing them with the resources they required to excel in their roles.

Every victory comes with its share of opposition. While I

was making strides with many agents, fellow supervisors, and even some members of management, one or two individuals resisted everything I represented. The opposition I faced here felt more than just typical; it had an almost supernatural quality. You could sense the animosity fueling their attacks, which wasn't directed only at me but at the principles I embodied.

I remained steadfast in my faith, undeterred by the personal assaults I faced. I understood that my struggle wasn't with people but with the spiritual forces at play. So, what was my next step? I turned to the Lord for guidance and sought support from others. To my surprise, I discovered that the supervisor I had encountered on my first day, alongside the admin manager, was also a fellow believer.

We made the choice to gather in each other's offices before every shift to come together in prayer. Our prayers were focused on the agents, our fellow supervisors, management, and their families. We poured our hearts into these prayers like never before, so much so that a few other supervisors expressed their desire to join us in this sacred time of intercession.

The situation grew more intense in the natural realm, revealing to us that our actions were influencing the supernatural. Our faith in the Lord stayed strong, unwavering in our dedication to intercessory prayer. It was the Holy Spirit, not us, who was saving souls from destruction.

Our dedication to the kingdom of God directly influenced our increasing commitment to our responsibility of national security. As supervisors, it was our duty to develop innovative strategies to address the evolving trends and tactics employed by criminal organizations. We consistently sought the guidance and direction of our Lord, even in this situation.

As my workload grew heavier, I found myself juggling multiple responsibilities, both in my professional life and within my pastoral duties at church. The demands of my job seemed to multiply, and the pressure began to weigh on me. Yet, despite the increasing challenges, I made a conscious decision to remain steadfast in my commitment to my church community. I understood that my role as a pastor was not just a title; it was a calling that required my unwavering dedication, even in the face of adversity.

Each Sunday, I poured my heart into delivering sermons that inspired and uplifted my congregation. I took the time to connect with individuals, offering support and guidance to those in need. It was not always easy, and at moments I felt overwhelmed and exhausted. However, I held onto the belief that my efforts, no matter how small, were significant in the grand scheme of God's plan.

Throughout this journey, I discovered a profound truth: When you remain committed to the little things, God rewards that faithfulness with greater blessings. I began to notice how my dedication to my pastoral duties, even when I felt stretched thin, opened doors to unexpected opportunities. Relationships deepened, and I witnessed transformations in the lives of those I served. The small acts of kindness and the consistent presence I offered began to bear fruit in ways I had not anticipated.

As I continued to prioritize my responsibilities at church, I found that my own spirit was rejuvenated. The joy of serving others became a source of strength that helped me navigate the pressures of my professional life. I realized that in committing to the little things—whether a simple prayer, a heartfelt conversation, or a moment of encouragement—I was not only fulfilling my role as a pastor but also nurturing my own faith.

In time, I experienced a shift in my perspective. The burdens I once felt began to feel lighter, and the blessings I received multiplied. I learned that God honors our faithfulness, and in return, He provides us with the strength and resilience to face our challenges. The more I invested in my church community, the more I felt a sense of purpose and fulfillment that transcended the pressures of my workload.

MESSENGER

Being a messenger comes with its challenges, especially when faced with rejection. It's essential to keep in mind that when someone turns you down, it's not a reflection of you personally; they are actually rejecting Christ. This is a profound lesson I had to learn.

While rejection can be painful, as a Christian, the reasons for that pain differ from those in the world. In the secular world, rejection often stings because it taps into our desire for acceptance and belonging. Yet, when you are rooted in Christ, your heart aches not for yourself, but because you long for others to know His love, mercy, and forgiveness.

I stayed committed to the journey that God laid out for me because of this very reason. Even in the face of opposition and rejection, I pressed on, having experienced both sides and understanding the depths of hopelessness. My love for humanity, instilled in me by God, drives me to embrace being seen as a fool for Christ in the eyes of the world.

During challenging times, the words He shared with me on that day when I was prepared to give everything for Him provided me with comfort: *You are my son, chosen to be a law enforcement officer. You are not just an officer that I have called to be my son.*

No matter your current role—be it a lawyer, police officer, educator, dedicated parent, or college student—God has a purpose for you right where you are. Your responsibility is to stay faithful and obedient to that calling. As a Christian, you are placed in your position for a significant reason; your divine appointment should not be taken lightly. Embrace your role, and trust that you are making a difference.

You are the only one who can connect with those around you; don't rely on others to fulfill the mission God has entrusted to you. This is why you are in that position and have experienced what you have. Your trials, insights, and perspective are invaluable tools that God has equipped you with to make a difference in the lives of those you encounter. Your presence in this specific environment is not a coincidence; it is a divine appointment.

Some people may not grasp the message, while others might outright dismiss it, regardless of the circumstances. In such moments, we must keep in mind that salvation is not ours to claim; it is a gift from our Lord Jesus. The person that sows seeds and the person who waters the seed hold no significance on their own; God is the one who brings growth.

The most fulfilling moments were when someone who

had repeatedly turned away from the message finally approached on their own terms. Naturally, I welcomed them with open arms. Often it was during their toughest days when they would question if God truly existed. These instances were rare, but when they occurred, I made sure not to preach to them. Instead, I focused on listening and being genuinely present for them. I believe this approach is far more effective than forcing religion or our opinions on them. In those quiet moments of simply being there, my presence spoke the loudest.

The core message is quite straightforward. God chose to become one of us and paid for the consequences of our sins on the cross. Why did He do this? Because of His immense love for us. So, why do we sometimes feel a sense of emptiness? It's due to sin. Sin creates a barrier between us and Him, and He came to mend that broken relationship by sacrificing Himself on the cross. Now, all we need to do is accept the free gift He has already provided. He promises to give us a new heart—one that understands Him, follows His ways, and desires to fulfill His will. How can we receive this new heart? By simply believing in His sacrifice, trusting in His forgiveness, and asking for His help and strength to avoid sinning against Him in the future.

The scriptures encourage us to be prepared in season and out of season, which means we should always be prepared to convey our message, even in challenging or uncomfortable situations. So, how can we remain prepared? By maintaining a close relationship with Him and telling others about the wonderful things He has done for you.

DO NOT GIVE UP!

There will be days when you will feel like throwing in the towel, moments when you'll think, "I don't need this!" Those are precisely the days when you must push through. They signify that you are closer to achieving a breakthrough.

You were placed in that area for a specific spiritual reason. Regardless of the challenges you face or how tough others may make it, your role is to create a spiritual impact. The more significant your influence, the tougher the opposition will become. The enemy will fight to maintain his territory.

The seriousness of this situation lies in the fact that an unseen battle is taking place, one that many people remain oblivious to. It's a struggle for souls; this isn't about religion or persuading anyone to join our social groups. The stakes are high, and if my willingness to follow through means even one soul reaches heaven, then it's all worthwhile!

Your mission is uniquely yours, crafted just for you. God

has positioned you there for a purpose, and He has faith in your ability to meet the challenge. The adversary will do everything he can to undermine you; trust me! He will attempt to tarnish your reputation with those you aim to connect with for Christ. While the obstacles you encounter may feel daunting at times, they also present chances for personal growth, learning, and strengthening your faith.

When you feel the weight of the task ahead, take comfort in the knowledge that you are not alone. You serve a God who is all-powerful, all-knowing, and ever-present. He is capable of moving mountains and transforming lives in ways we cannot even begin to imagine. Trust in His plan and lean on His strength, for He has equipped you with everything you need to succeed.

As you step forward in faith, remember that your efforts, no matter how small they may seem, can have a profound impact. Each conversation, each act of kindness, and each moment of connection can ripple outward, touching lives in ways you may never fully comprehend. Embrace the challenge with courage and determination, knowing that you are fulfilling a purpose greater than yourself.

Therefore, step up to what God has called you to with confidence. Embrace the mission that God has entrusted to you, and remember that with Him, all things are possible. Your willingness to engage with those around you can be the catalyst for change, healing, and transformation in your sphere of influence.

Throughout my journey of faith and service, I've come to understand a profound truth: God doesn't ask us to fulfill His will through our own efforts alone. Instead, He empowers us with the Holy Spirit, who dwells within us once we accept Jesus as our Savior. This transformation is what the scriptures refer to as the new heart, as mentioned in Ezekiel and Joel. A particular verse that resonates with me about depending on God's Spirit rather than our own abilities is found in Isaiah 40:31: "But those who hope in the LORD will renew their strength. They will soar on wings like eagles; they will run and not grow weary, they will walk and not be faint."

An eagle relies on ascending air currents to elevate itself, spreading its wings wide to glide effortlessly rather than flapping about like chickens or turkeys. Similarly, we are encouraged to emulate eagles by trusting in the Holy Spirit to raise us to greater heights, avoiding the exhausting struggle of relying solely on our own strength to make progress.

When life feels confusing and unclear, it's important not to lean solely on your own understanding. Instead, place your complete trust in the Lord, and He will lead you on the right path. The scriptures assure us that the Holy Spirit will guide us and show us the way to go. We are not abandoned; He has promised to be with us always. Draw strength from His promises and continue to move forward, regardless of what you can or cannot see. Keep pushing ahead and never lose hope, for in due time, your perseverance will yield a bountiful harvest.

chapter six

TWO TEAMS

"Obey me, and I will be your God and you will be my people.
Walk in obedience to all I command you, that it may go well
with you."

JEREMIAH 7:23

My Nineveh turned out to be a true blessing. During my time
in what I viewed as a wilderness, I gained a wealth of
knowledge and insight. This station was known for being one
of the busiest in the country, as well as one of the most
demanding. While the journey of growth can be physically
painful, the spiritual rewards far surpass the discomfort.

Before ascending to the throne, King David learned the importance of responsibility through his role as a shepherd in his youth. His brothers often mocked and belittled him for this humble position. Yet, David stayed committed to his sheep, demonstrating unwavering dedication despite the ridicule. In 1 Samuel chapter 17, we witness David's true character and the deep care he had for his flock; for him, being a shepherd was not merely a job but a heartfelt commitment.

David discovered through tending to his sheep that God was always by his side. When faced with challenges, whether from a lion or a bear, David relied on the Lord rather than his own strength to confront the threat and protect what was entrusted to him. God rewards a heart like David's—one that is not selfish or self-serving, but rather willing to lay down his life for those he loves and cares for. Similarly, when we open our hearts to allow God to work within us and embrace a spirit of genuine service to others, that is when He entrusts us with greater responsibilities. This transformation cannot be achieved on our own; it occurs when we learn to trust and obey Him in the small things.

As a canine handler, I faced some tough days, but I didn't realize at the time that those experiences were shaping me for the future. Much like how our drill instructors got us ready through the challenges of boot camp or how our parents taught us responsibility through chores, our loving Father is also preparing us for what lies ahead.

OBEDIENCE IS BETTER THAN SACRIFICE

During my time as a handler, I experienced two distinct types of teams, each presenting its own set of challenges and rewards. My first partner, the Belgian Malinois K9 Rudie, was not only obedient but also incredibly affectionate. He thrived on both work and play, responding to my commands without a moment's hesitation. The bond we shared was exceptionally strong; we learned to trust and rely on each other completely. Together, we achieved considerable success in our endeavors. Working with Rudie felt less like a job and more like an exciting adventure that I eagerly anticipated every day. His unwavering obedience and loving nature truly highlighted my achievements as a handler.

My second partner, the Dutch shepherd named Bunker, had a strong will and a tendency to follow his own instincts. During our time together, we often clashed, which made our work less effective. Every day with K9 Bunker by my side seemed to bring a new level of stress.

This dog never fully developed a bond of trust with me. Despite having a keen sense of smell that surpassed my first dog's, he wasn't as effective in his role. Rudie, on the other hand, thrived because of his submissive demeanor. He figured out that by simply sticking close to his dad, he could get his toy much quicker.

When we choose to submit to God not through obligation but through love, we discover that this is the source of everything we have sought throughout our lives: true love, hope, peace, and provision. Rudie realized that by staying close to me, he would receive all these blessings and even more. The Bible refers to this as walking in the spirit.

The flesh, or the act of walking in our own will, promises the same blessings and even more. However, the reality is that when we choose to go our own way, we often find ourselves poor, miserable, and isolated. This was true for K9 Bunker; despite his outward appearance suggesting otherwise, he did not enjoy or produce the fruits of those promised blessings.

Although hard to believe, this lesson has surfaced repeatedly in my life, serving as a powerful reminder of the repercussions that stem from our own choices. When we engage in habitual sin, we are essentially opting for death. God presented a similar choice to the nation of Israel in the book of Deuteronomy, where He laid out the options of life or death. He went further by detailing the consequences of each path, ultimately encouraging them to select life.

Before we came to know God, we were trapped in the cycle of our own sinful choices and their consequences, lacking the strength to break free or make different decisions. Much like K9 Bunker, whose animal instincts prevented him from obeying my commands due to his selfish desires, our own flesh led us astray before we experienced a true encounter with the living God.

When we welcome God into our lives and open our hearts to Jesus, we gain the strength to conquer sin and embrace the victory He has called us to. This journey isn't one we can navigate alone; we rely on the Holy Spirit to guide us in living in obedience to His will.

THE HARVEST

My time as a dog handler provided me with invaluable lessons in personal growth and leadership. I learned that my commitment to each dog, regardless of their temperament—be it submissive or otherwise—was what truly mattered. This lesson in faithfulness to my role as a handler helped shape my character.

Staying true to our divine calling, regardless of opposition or the actions of others, demonstrates our unwavering commitment to God. In doing so, you will undoubtedly reap the rewards of your faithfulness.

I've experienced this lesson repeatedly throughout my life. During my time in Nineveh, I had been dedicatedly working as a supervisor, not seeking a promotion in the near future, when a managerial position became available. While the assignment was tough, I was truly enjoying my role as a supervisor and felt like I was finally achieving significant progress with my team. I was reminded of David, who remained loyal to his flock without any expectations, until God sent the prophet Samuel to anoint him as the king of Israel.

When this managerial role opened up, one of my closest friends, who was a fellow supervisor, urged me to apply. I was skeptical about my chances, especially with other more experienced supervisors applying for the same position. However, he motivated me by saying that if the job was meant for me, I would land it regardless of the competition. He added, what's the worst that could happen? You might actually get it!

On that day, we both decided to apply for the job since there were multiple openings available. To be honest, I was quite content with my current situation, feeling grateful for where I was in life. A promotion wasn't on my radar, especially considering how abundantly I had already been blessed.

About three weeks later, my friend and I were summoned to the office of the agent in charge at the station. I vividly recall him asking us where we envisioned ourselves in the coming year. I replied, "In management, sir." He then inquired why I aspired to that role. My friend chimed in, expressing his desire to lead others positively. I added that I wanted to make a meaningful impact on people's lives by utilizing the knowledge I had gained from my mentors. The agent in charge then congratulated us and welcomed us to management.

The other managers came forward to congratulate us too. My friend and I were left in awe, unable to find the words. Soon after, we were assigned to our new unit and instructed to report the following day. That night, sleep eluded me. I kept expressing my gratitude to the Lord, still in disbelief over the incredible turn of events. I never would have thought such a thing could happen, not in a million years. As Luke 18:27 says, "What is impossible with man is possible with God."

God had been equipping me for this role. Over the years, I was frequently asked to step into an acting manager position, particularly on weekends when some managers were off or on leave. So, finally receiving the permanent manager position felt like a natural progression rather than something new.

A remarkable aspect of our Lord is that He faithfully

equips His people in advance. Take King David as an example; before he confronted Goliath as a young shepherd, he had already triumphed over a lion and a bear while caring for his father's flock. David's confidence stemmed not from his own abilities but from the mighty God he faithfully served. This is evident in 1 Samuel, where David approaches King Saul and declares that the Lord who saved him from the lion and the bear would also deliver him from the Philistine.

HE WILL NEVER FORSAKE US

One of the best pieces of advice I ever got from a senior manager was to avoid being a people pleaser. He emphasized that trying to make everyone happy is a losing battle; instead, he urged me to focus on doing what is right and fair, and that approach would guide me successfully.

As a pastor, I quickly learned this lesson and realized that trying to make everyone happy can be incredibly overwhelming. The key is to be honest and genuine in your approach. Along the journey, you will inevitably encounter people who are unable to understand your decisions, and no matter your efforts, you won't be able to satisfy them all. As a leader, I've learned the importance of focusing on what is right and beneficial for the greater good and to keep moving forward. Especially when following a directive from the Lord, you may find that those who aren't aligned with the Spirit of God will often stand against you, regardless of your actions.

In my experience, the more God elevates you, the more solitude you may encounter—not that you choose to leave people behind; rather, they tend to drift away. I first noticed this shift when I dedicated my life to the Lord. Many of my old friends, or rather, most of my colleagues who used to invite me out for drinks, completely stopped reaching out once I embraced my faith. This pattern repeated itself when I advanced to a supervisory role and then to management.

No matter the situation, I had to place my trust in the Lord and focus on fulfilling His purpose rather than my own desires. The adversary will always seek to undermine your confidence and instill doubt about whether God genuinely placed you in your current position. The enemy's goal is to render you ineffective in advancing the kingdom of God. He may either inflate your ego, whispering, "Look at how amazing you are, how successful you've become through your own efforts," or he might belittle your worth, suggesting that you don't deserve your current position and urging you to abandon your quest to make a difference.

Promotion ultimately comes from the Lord, and your current position is a result of His guidance. All that we have achieved and everything we possess is due to His grace. So, the real question is: How are you using the blessings God has given you? Are you sharing those blessings with others, or have you stepped away from your responsibilities? In the Marine Corps, we were taught a key principle during guard duty: It is the fifth general order, "To quit our post only when properly relieved."

As Christians, we should only leave our posts when we are properly relieved. Just like the Israelites in the wilderness, who were guided by a cloud during the day and a fire at night for warmth and protection in the cold desert, we too must wait for God's direction. As long as they followed God's lead, they were safe and cared for. However, if they chose to move ahead of Him, or lagged, they risked losing that divine protection.

When we stray from God's will, we also lose His protective covering. Within that covering is where we find safety and care. Psalm 91:1–2 reminds us: "Whoever dwells in the shelter of the Most High will rest in the shadow of the Almighty. I will say of the Lord, 'He is my refuge and my fortress, my God, in whom I trust.'"

Throughout the years, I have felt God's guidance in my life. Even during moments when I felt utterly alone, I realized that those were the times He was closest to me. In recognizing

His presence and dedicating my plans to Him, I have found the clearest direction for my path.

During my time as a manager, I faced difficult situations, particularly when supervisors or the troops encountered issues they had never faced before. At those times, I found myself in the role of the go-to person for everyone seeking direction. My response was to seek wisdom from God, and without fail, I received insight from Him each time.

I recall when I was younger, if I faced a challenge or had a concern, I would confidently turn to my dad, certain he would have the right answer or solution. I really miss that about him. Even now, when I encounter a problem or need someone to confide in, I find myself reaching for the phone to call him, only to remember that he's with our Lord in heaven. The comforting part is that our heavenly Father has assured us that He will never leave or forsake us, and if we need wisdom, direction, and comfort, we can simply ask Him.

DIVINE INTERVENTION

I truly enjoyed my time as a manager. By the third year, I was blessed to be teamed up with my close friend, the very person who had encouraged me to pursue this role. It really makes a huge difference when you and your partner are in sync. Perhaps our strong connection stemmed from the fact that we were quite similar. He had also served in the US Marines and had encountered many of the same conflicts I had. A dedicated family man, he cherished his loved ones deeply, and our aspirations and dreams were very much in harmony.

As I reflect on my life as I get older, I see that God has consistently brought a Jonathan into my journey. In the Bible, Jonathan and David shared a deep friendship, always looking out for one another. No matter where I found myself, the Lord provided me with someone I could rely on to help me navigate the difficulties I encountered. This support was evident during my time in the Marines, while I served in the Sheriff's Department, and throughout my career in federal law enforcement. I have never been alone on this path.

Each day I headed to work, I found it to be a genuinely enjoyable experience. While we certainly faced our share of challenging days in terms of workload, the presence of the right people made a positive impact. The morale within our unit was at an all-time high, thanks to the supportive supervisors and dedicated troops we had.

Everything seemed to be going wonderfully. The church I was serving at was flourishing, my boys were getting older, and my marriage was in the best shape it had been in years. My wife and I had made the choice that this would be our retirement spot, where we would settle down and raise our kids. We enjoyed the town and the community, which wasn't a large city or overly tiny; it was the perfect size for raising our boys.

Typically, when agents attain the managerial level that I had been blessed to achieve, they tend to retire upon reaching that milestone. My intention had been to remain in the area and after a couple of years retire and continue my pastoral work at the church or wherever God guided me.

But God apparently had other intentions for us. During that time, my mother-in-law fell seriously ill. She lived a few hours away, and my wife and her sisters took turns driving their mother to medical appointments. My wife often had to make the long journey alone to pick up her mother and then transport her to various doctor's visits, sometimes even in a different city. This continued for a couple years, and I found myself quite anxious about her traveling alone.

I turned to prayer, seeking guidance from God on how I could support my wife and spare her from those long drives. Then the thought struck me: I should look for a new position or a transfer closer to where my wife and I grew up. I remember the moment I shared this idea with my wife. Her face lit up with a big smile. "That's exactly what I've been thinking!" she exclaimed. We both laughed, recognizing this as a clear sign from God, especially since we rarely agree on anything.

The choice was tough, especially since everything seemed to be going perfectly, but I made it nonetheless. The very next day, I started applying for jobs closer to our hometowns. I was even open to taking a step back to a supervisor role if it meant being closer to my childhood home.

Just then, another manager came into my office and asked what I was up to. I shared my situation with him, and he inquired whether I had submitted a memorandum for a hardship transfer to headquarters. I had no idea that option even existed. He offered to send me some sample memos, since he had gone through a similar situation. I looked up to the heavens and smiled, feeling grateful to God for the way He always provides support just when I need it.

About six months later, during a day shift still working the same job, I recall making the rounds with my fellow supervisors to ensure everything was running smoothly in the field. The agent in charge of the station approached and asked a pivotal question: Would I be interested in taking a job at sector headquarters?

I quickly replied, "Absolutely, sir! I would love to go to

sector headquarters." Then I inquired about when I would need to report. "Immediately," he said. I shook his hand and expressed my gratitude repeatedly.

The astonishing reality of this scenario is that landing a permanent role at headquarters is almost impossible. Countless individuals have tried, yet few have seen any success. In this vocation and many others, if you haven't networked, as in building connections while advancing in your career, your chances of moving forward on your own are typically slim.

Typically, it's essential to have someone in your corner— someone you've collaborated with in the past or shared experiences with—who has advanced in their career and can support your ascent or endorse your capabilities. I, however, had no network. Securing the position at headquarters was truly a divine intervention, as I lacked any connections to advocate for me—except God!

The sale of our house was truly remarkable as well. As soon as we put it on the market, the first person who came to see it showed interest, made an offer, and finalized the purchase—all in under a two-week span. This was truly another miracle that had God's signature all over it. In all our experiences, we had never seen a home sell so quickly. We even double-checked with the buyer to ensure she was certain about her decision, just to clarify any potential misunderstanding. The best part? We received an offer that was double what we originally paid for the house.

My wife and I hurried to get everything packed up, but this time we had eighteen years' worth of stuff to sort through, along with our two wonderful kids that we've been blessed with—a big change from when we first moved in and our entire life fit into just one box! Now, we found ourselves needing to rent a big moving truck, which turned into a fun adventure for our two boys.

This entire journey had been an emotional whirlwind. We felt immense joy at the prospect of being nearer to our family, but also a deep sadness in saying goodbye to our church family and cherished friends from work. We would truly miss this place, where we witnessed God make the impossible possible. This town and church were where our humble beginnings took root, and we watched our children grow up surrounded by love and faith.

We knew we had to trust in the path that God set before us. When I shared the news with the congregation, their sadness mirrored my own, yet they were understanding. Much like David the shepherd boy who entrusted his sheep to a reliable caretaker, I too found comfort in knowing that God had provided someone who would care for them with the same love.

chapter seven

DOWN THE LEASH

"But the fruit of the Spirit is love, joy, peace, forbearance, kindness, goodness, faithfulness, gentleness and self-control. Against such things there is no law."

GALATIANS 5:22–23

At the K9 handler academy, we learned a remarkable insight that many people are unaware of. We discovered that all our emotions as humans can travel directly down the leash and be sensed by the dog. The instructors explained that the leash functions like an antenna. Our feelings—be it frustration, fear, anxiety, confusion, confidence, encouragement, or any other emotion we experience throughout the day—can significantly influence the dog's performance in a positive or negative way.

As I began my journey as a canine handler, some moments during training tested my patience. I often felt frustrated, which prompted my instructor to advise me to put my dog away. Initially, I was puzzled by this suggestion, especially since it often occurred halfway through a field search training exercise. However, he clarified that when I was in a negative state of mind, it affected my dog's performance, and they wouldn't work as effectively afterward.

Some dogs may withdraw entirely when sensing their partner's distress, while others might become distracted or reflect their handler's emotions, leading to irritability and reduced effectiveness in their tasks.

One of the most effective strategies I've discovered for dealing with frustration as a handler was to follow the advice of my instructor and place the dog in his kennel and take a short walk. This simple act allowed me to step back and reflect on my feelings.

Surprisingly, I've found this approach beneficial in various roles, whether as a manager, a minister, or a husband. Nowadays, when I feel overwhelmed, I still take that walk, but my focus has shifted. Instead of simply reassessing my emotions, I use that time to pray to God, seeking peace and guidance on how to move forward.

Before Christ came into my life, I didn't realize how my actions, whether positive or negative, affected the people around me, just like when I was a handler, and my emotions traveled straight down the leash. We can only share what we possess within ourselves. At that time, all I had to give was a mix of hate, selfishness, anger, resentment, insecurity, jealousy, and many other negative emotions. But when the Lord transformed my heart, filling it with love for Him and for others, everything changed.

As a chaplain, peer support member, manager, and minister, I often prioritized the needs of others over my own. To me, this was the clearest sign of God's presence in my life. Without Christ in our hearts, it's difficult to genuinely put others first. We are all born with sin, which taints our hearts and influences our actions. On our own, we tend to be selfish, unkind, and inconsiderate.

The key to transformation lies in the Holy Spirit. He is the source that brings joy, peace, love, kindness, goodness, faithfulness, gentleness, and self-control into our lives. Through Christ I have discovered the ability to truly love and care for others.

THE ALPHA

My leadership graciously granted me a couple weeks off before I started at my new duty station. I was genuinely thankful for this time, as it gave us the opportunity to reconnect with family we hadn't seen in a long time because of the distance. One of our relatives even kindly offered us a place to stay while we looked for a home or thought about building a new one.

We gladly took them up on their offer since we didn't have any other plans besides putting our belongings in storage. Shortly after, we began our hunt for a new home. After several months of looking without success, we decided that building our own home would be the best choice.

The long-awaited day to check in at headquarters had finally come. I felt a mix of excitement and nerves as I arrived for duty. Upon reporting, I learned that my boss was on annual leave. The only person I got to meet that first day was the manager I was set to replace. To my surprise, he was still around, having chosen to stay until someone took over his position before retiring.

As I introduced myself, the first thing he said was, "Are you ready to travel?" Taken aback, I asked, "Where to?" He went on to explain that one of the teams I was going to lead had to embark on a three-day journey to attend a national program conference in Washington, DC, where they would be representing the sector.

When I returned home from work, I nervously told my wife all about it, and her response was, "Oh, it's just a three-day trip. Okay." The whole experience caught me by surprise; I hadn't anticipated traveling so soon, if at all. I distinctly recall asking God, "What are you up to, Lord?"

During my initial encounters with some of my travel companions, I observed a common curiosity regarding my background. Everyone was eager to learn about my tenure, my previous experiences, and the areas in which I specialized. I interpreted their curiosity to mean they were comparing themselves to me. Many of the staff were quite junior, and I gathered that most of them were focused on climbing the ladder and establishing their reputation by being at HQ. A new person joining seemed to create a sense of competition, as if they feared losing their chance for promotion.

The distinction between walking in the flesh and walking in the Spirit is significant. I've discovered that when you walk with God and cultivate a genuine relationship with Him, nothing can truly threaten you. You realize that God is the author and finisher of your faith. He guides your steps and determines your path. You learn that whatever door He opens no man can close, and whatever door He shuts, no man can open. God is the one who promotes, and our role is to obey and follow His guidance. By doing so, I've consistently experienced His blessings. I have experienced challenging times along the way, but by remaining steadfast, others have been blessed and I've always emerged stronger.

A few colleagues didn't seem to be caught up in a competitive mindset; they were simply grateful to be there and radiated genuine friendliness. I formed close friendships with these individuals.

I have always believed in treating everyone with equal respect, a valuable lesson my father shared with me when I began my journey in law enforcement. I can still recall the moment he imparted this wisdom, saying, "Son, always be fair and respectful to everyone. It doesn't matter where someone comes from or who they are; we are all God's children."

PSALM 23

I completely understood what my dad meant. I've always believed in treating everyone with kindness, but I've also learned that there are times when a leader needs to take a strong stance. The Bible puts it well in Matthew 10:16: "I am sending you out like sheep among wolves. Therefore be as shrewd as snakes and as innocent as doves."

Before I began my journey at my new job, I received a warning from my heavenly Father through a dream, advising me to be careful in my interactions with certain individuals. When I arrived at headquarters, I was unprepared for the confrontations that awaited me. Clearly, these challenges had a spiritual dimension. Throughout my career, whether as an agent, a dog handler, or a supervisor and manager, I had encountered many tough situations in the field, but the opposition I faced this time was truly unprecedented.

I remained faithful to my work, and like clockwork, my Lord blessed me with not only one, but several brothers in the faith who prayed alongside me and supported me through every challenge. We always made it a priority to pray at the beginning of each day. Our prayers included everyone from the chief to the agents in the field and their families.

When God guides us to a specific location, it's not just about the tasks we perform; it's about being a beacon of light and the salt of the earth in our community, as the Scriptures instruct us. Often, we as Christians lose sight of our true purpose. We overlook that we are placed where we are to impact the kingdom positively. Our presence isn't for personal benefit but for the growth of the kingdom. We are supposed to be like firefighters, saving souls from the flames of hell.

When we become too absorbed in our own lives, we often lose sight of what God has intended for us. Everyone experiences this at some time or another, whether due to our own ambitions, financial struggles, health issues, or any other challenges life throws our way. In these moments, we must remain strong and vigilant.

In the Bible book of Judges is a tale about Gideon, whose name means "Great Warrior." When God called upon Gideon, he was hiding out from fear of the enemy. Despite being the least in his family, Gideon was God's selection to confront the Midianites, the enemy of that time.

Gideon began with an army of 33,000 soldiers, but God instructed him to send home anyone who was afraid, and 10,000 left. God wanted to demonstrate that the victory would come from His power, not their own. Facing an enemy force of 135,000 with only 22,000 of his own soldiers remaining, God informed Gideon that this number was still too large.

He then provided Gideon with additional guidance, instructing him to lead the soldiers to the river so they could hydrate. He asked Gideon to distinguish between those who drank by lapping water like dogs and those who knelt to drink. Out of the group, three hundred used their hands to scoop water, lapping it up like dogs, while the others knelt down to take a drink. God instructed Gideon to dismiss all but the three hundred who scooped up the water.

The Lord assured Gideon that with just three hundred men, He would hand the Midianites over to him. This victory demonstrated that God can triumph over the enemy, regardless of the numbers involved. Ultimately, the battle is in the hands of our Lord.

I genuinely believe that God selected the three hundred to remain because they were the ones who stayed watchful while drinking water. Those who looked down while drinking lost their focus. A true warrior remains attentive, whether in leisure or on duty; 1 Peter 5:8: "Be alert and of sober mind. Your enemy the devil prowls around like a roaring lion looking for someone to devour."

RELENTLESS

The adversary is relentless, fully aware that his time is limited and conscious of where he is headed. The devil doesn't play fair; he will resort to any means necessary to prevent you from embracing Jesus as your Savior. He understands that once you invite Christ into your heart, the truth will be unveiled to you. Only God can reveal His truth, and He does so through the Holy Spirit. This journey isn't merely about religion; it's about you accepting His salvation and allowing Him to reign as Lord of your life so you can truly perceive the truth.

The enemy is a clever strategist. If he can't reach us directly because we are firmly anchored in Christ, he will attempt to influence those who are closest to us. If that fails, he will target those around us who haven't fully committed their hearts to the Lord. These individuals are more susceptible and can be used to disrupt God's plan for others to find their way to Christ.

He has been employing this strategy from the very start, and we can see a clear example of it in Genesis 3, often referred to as the fall of man. In this story, the devil comes to Eve in the form of a serpent. It's interesting to note that the enemy doesn't come to us as something strange, but rather as something we recognize. Eve was accustomed to the animals in the Garden of Eden, so for a serpent to approach her felt familiar and comfortable.

Satan chose not to confront Adam directly. Instead, he deceived Eve, leading her to accept a falsehood, which made it simpler for her to disobey God. Once he had influenced Eve, he realized that reaching Adam through her would be a much easier task. Sometimes, the devil may choose to approach us in a roundabout way, using someone we care about and trust, rather than facing us head-on. This tactic can make the impact of the attack even stronger.

The adversary attempted a similar tactic with our Lord shortly after His baptism at the age of thirty. Jesus was taken into the wilderness for forty days, where He fasted and faced temptation on three separate occasions. However, our Lord countered each temptation by speaking the Word of God.

Adam and Eve faced a crucial moment when they chose not to uphold God's word. Instead of relying on His strength, they attempted to handle temptation on their own, which ultimately led to their downfall. This choice had far-reaching consequences, impacting all of humanity. Every child born after the fall inherits this sinful nature. This is why we need a Savior—someone who was born free from sin. That Savior is Jesus, God who came to earth as a man, born of a virgin, crucified on the cross for our sins.

STAND FIRM

The more challenges we face, the sweeter the triumph that awaits us. Our new home was finally under construction, and my family and I were excited. We had never experienced owning a newly built house before. We discovered a lovely spot in a gated community, which turned out to be a bit farther from my job than we had expected, but we adapted. One of the first things we did as we began to embrace our new life in the community was to search for a church.

We checked out a few nearby churches, but none felt quite right. I turned to my Lord in prayer, seeking guidance on what to do next. I wondered if He wanted me to start a new ministry, assist another pastor, or something else entirely. Both my wife and I felt led to continue searching for a church. Our prayer was straightforward regarding our new church: we asked the Lord for a place that wasn't too big or too small, one that had a children's and youth ministry. Most importantly, we prayed that the pastor would love God above all else, knowing that if the pastor had that love, everything else would fall into place.

I started searching for a church online and kept finding myself drawn to the same one, not too far from our house. We decided to visit on a Wednesday evening. I recall it was November, as we entered to find round tables set up from their Thanksgiving luncheon held the previous Sunday. The moment I took a seat, I felt a gentle whisper from the Lord saying, "This is it; this is where I have called you."

As the pastor concluded his sermon, my wife and I exchanged glances and simultaneously felt a deep sense of belonging—this was our home. This church offered everything we had hoped and prayed for and even more. Now, over a decade later, we continue to serve faithfully in the place where God led us. This ministry has been a true blessing in our lives; it's where our boys have grown up and learned about our Lord. This church has genuinely been a divine gift. Like any journey, we've faced a few challenges, but nothing has ever swayed us from following God's path.

Christians must be firmly anchored in a Bible-believing church where they can thrive. Challenges and temptations will inevitably arise, and without a solid foundation in the truth, you may find yourself swept away, much like a sandcastle eroded by the relentless tide.

The anticipated attack from the adversary indeed occurred, this time employing a skilled individual who, through their compelling influence, persuaded senior management to reorganize all programs at headquarters to serve this person's interests. During this transition, the person seized the chance to remove individuals of faith. Although the reorganization was done discreetly, the goal was evident, as I, along with several fellow Christian brothers, found ourselves reassigned to a different location.

This situation felt all too familiar; when the enemy strikes, it often appears to be the end of the line, with no escape in sight. Yet, I stood firm and resolute, unwavering in my faith. I was confident in whom I placed my trust, knowing that nothing is impossible for my God. The adversary made every effort to sabotage God's plan, yet he overlooked the fact that it is God who holds ultimate control, not man.

Upon receiving my newly assigned office space, a government vehicle, and my schedule for the new workplace, I received a call from a senior manager inquiring about my whereabouts. I informed him that I was at the location specified by the other chief. He then asked if I would be interested in returning to headquarters to work under his leadership. Without a moment's pause, I enthusiastically responded, "Absolutely, sir! I would be thrilled to come back."

What the enemy meant for harm, God transformed into something good! Stay strong in your faith; the battle continues until God declares it finished. Time and again, God has shown His faithfulness in my life, and He will do the same for you if you fully surrender to Him.

chapter eight

THE NOSE KNOWS

"And without faith it is impossible to please God, because anyone who comes to him must believe that he exists and that he rewards those who earnestly seek him."

HEBREWS 11:6

At times, God may lead you on a path that seems confusing to our human understanding. During these moments, it's essential to rely on trust rather than what is visible. As you deepen your relationship with the Lord through scripture and spend quality time in prayer, He will gradually unveil more of Himself to you, reinforcing your ability to trust Him. You'll come to realize that God is faithful and will bring to fruition the promises made in your life.

The Bible teaches us that God bestows a measure of faith upon each of His children. As we journey alongside Him, our faith grows through various experiences. Just like in any aspect of life, He begins with small steps, gradually expanding our encounters with Him over time. For instance, David's faith was strengthened when he confronted a lion and a bear before ultimately facing Goliath.

The Israelites missed an important lesson during their time in the wilderness. After freeing them from slavery in Egypt, God aimed to strengthen their trust in Him through various experiences. Unfortunately, they were too focused on their own needs and desires to see that God wanted to show them His good intentions. The Lord assures us in Jeremiah 29:11, "For I know the plans I have for you," declares the LORD, "plans to prosper you and not to harm you, plans to give you hope and a future."

God's ultimate intention was to guide His people to the promised land. However, before leading them there, He aimed to uncover what was in their hearts. As stated in Deuteronomy 8:2, "Remember how the LORD your God led you all the way in the wilderness these forty years, to humble and test you in order to know what was in your heart, whether or not you would keep his commands." For our benefit, God will not bring us to our promised land too soon, as it could turn into a curse rather than a blessing.

God cares more about our eternal well-being than our temporary comfort. If leading us to a better future requires us to face some discomfort now, He will permit that in our lives. During challenging times we genuinely discover what truly is in our hearts.

NOT A BLIND FAITH

God isn't asking you to follow Him blindly; instead, He desires a close and personal relationship with each of us. He wants the chance to demonstrate His truth in your life. His aim is to reveal Himself to us fully, on a personal level. Jesus didn't come to establish a religion; He came to mend the relationship with humanity that was broken in the Garden of Eden due to sin.

An instructor plays a crucial role in the selection process at the K9 training facility by matching handlers with dogs that suit their personalities. This pairing is essential for creating strong, effective teams. The significance of this compatibility lies in the fact that handlers and dogs will spend a considerable amount of time together, making it necessary for their relationship to thrive.

If a team is not compatible, no matter how hard the handler works to be effective, success will be elusive. The daily grind will become frustrating, and the team won't achieve the results it could if they were working well together. Similarly, someone attempting to fulfill God's work without the guidance of the Holy Spirit, whether in their own life or in the lives of others, is engaging in unproductive efforts. This often leads to frustration and eventual burnout, which is a common outcome of religion. God longs for a personal relationship with you and wants to fill you with His Spirit, empowering you to accomplish His will through His strength rather than your own. This connection will bring vitality to your life and those around you.

A key lesson we learn as dog handlers is the importance of building a solid connection with our K9 companions. This bond is essential for creating a strong team. Additionally, we are taught to place our trust in our dogs. Without that trust, achieving success as a team becomes quite challenging. This connection is crucial when working with dogs; without trusting your dog, your dog won't feel secure in trusting you. Bonding should happen organically, not through coercion.

One of the key activities we learn to strengthen our bond

with our dogs is simply taking them for a leisurely walk each day. Engaging in a game of fetch is another great way to connect, and surprisingly, having casual conversations with them—without any commands—can be beneficial too. An essential lesson we learn is to keep commands to a minimum when reinforcing obedience. Overdoing it can lead to stress for our furry friends.

Quality time is what truly matters, rather than just the amount of time spent together, which is true for any relationship. It's not the number of hours that counts, but the meaningful moments you share. Through spending quality time, your dog will learn to trust and respond better to you.

Building a strong bond and trust with your dog simplifies the job significantly. A dog's sense of smell is incredibly powerful. When trained to detect specific scents—be it explosives, narcotics, or even in search and rescue missions to find lost individuals or objects—a dog's nose is truly reliable. An unsuccessful search is often due to the handler's approach. Once you establish trust with your dog and learn to read the dog's body posture accurately, everything else will naturally align.

As our faith in the Lord deepens through our unwavering commitment to Him, we may encounter challenges along the way. However, these experiences will teach us to rely on Him with confidence rather than relying solely on ourselves.

DO NOT TURN BACK

When you place your trust in the Lord, hold firmly to the progress you've made in your spiritual journey. Hebrews 10:39 reminds us that "we are not of those who shrink back and are destroyed, but of those who have faith and preserve their souls" (ESV). In God's kingdom, what may appear to be a setback can actually be a triumph. In due time, He will show you that had He granted that urgent prayer you fervently sought, it might have led to your downfall.

Even though I faced a setback when I was moved from HQ and later asked to return, the entire experience turned out to be a blessing in disguise. On my first day back, the chief who had invited me to join his team entrusted me with overseeing teams and units that were truly impactful and made a significant difference in national security. In addition, I got to work with amazing colleagues. God clearly had a hand in this, as I found myself back in the very building from which I had been removed, but this time in a larger office with more space and a stunning view. Anyone who witnessed this journey would undoubtedly agree that it was all God's doing.

I could have easily become resentful and held onto anger

toward those who initially had me removed from HQ, but I chose to place my trust in the Lord and forgive. I was completely confident that God would bring good out of the entire situation. I refused to let the enemy undermine my faith; instead, I resolved to stay faithful to my Lord, no matter where or with whom He placed me.

Oil can only be extracted from an olive when it is ripe, fully matured, and gently pressed. Similarly, I felt that God was getting me ready for another significant role. I could sense the preparation taking place, and while the process can be painful, I understood that the outcome would make it all worthwhile.

While I concentrated on my tasks as a manager, I noticed that arrests and apprehensions had surged, due to policies enacted by the administration in power at that time. It's fascinating to observe how a leader's decision, whether for good or for bad, can create a notable impact.

Edmund Burke, an influential Irish statesman from the eighteenth century, is often credited with the powerful saying, "Evil prevails when good men fail to act." This statement resonates deeply with me! Throughout my lifetime, I have seen this truth unfold from politics to even the church at large. We are called to be a righteous influence within our circles. When we neglect to pray for our leaders, our communities, our youth, and our children, we inadvertently allow the enemy to gain a foothold in our lives.

The adversary is fully aware of his purpose, as highlighted in John 10:10: "The thief comes only to steal and kill and destroy." He is merciless and will strike from every angle. No one is safe from his attacks—he targets the elderly, the young, and everyone in between, showing no favoritism. His strategy is straightforward: focus on destroying the family, and the community will crumble; weaken the community, and the nation will follow.

You are appointed as the watchman on the wall, and it begins with you. Stay focused on what truly matters and avoid distractions. Do not revert to your former life or old habits. Remain steadfast in your mission, as many souls rely on your commitment.

Nehemiah served as a cupbearer for King Artaxerxes I of Persia during a time when the nation of Israel was in exile in Babylonia. Whenever he encountered fellow Jews returning from Jerusalem, he would inquire about the state of their community, particularly those who had returned to rebuild. He learned that the walls of Jerusalem were in ruins and its gates had been destroyed by fire (Nehemiah 1:3).

Nehemiah was deeply saddened. He could have easily chosen to be selfish and overlook everything happening around him, especially since he held a prominent position. Instead, he chose to seek the Lord's guidance regarding the situation.

Nehemiah was inspired to assist in the rebuilding and restoration of Jerusalem. Upon his arrival, the enemies in the vicinity quickly mocked and threatened him multiple times, warning that he would regret continuing his work. However, Nehemiah chose to ignore their taunts and instead brought his concerns to God, as noted in Nehemiah 4:4.

Nehemiah pressed on with the project, assigning workers to rebuild the wall while wielding weapons in their other hand. He urged them to stay alert against any threats. Despite the ongoing intimidation from the enemy, Nehemiah and his fellow Jews remained steadfast and completed the task in only fifty-two days, overcoming all opposition.

This passage from the Bible serves as an excellent illustration of what God can achieve through someone committed to His purpose. You can be sure that the enemy will strike; he aims to prevent you from completing the mission God has given you. He understands that if he can undermine us individually, he is not only affecting us but also everyone we are meant to influence.

A TIME OF DARKNESS

I realized quite clearly that my task at headquarters was crucial, and I understood that this was why the enemy had attempted to remove me from that position multiple times. When you stay focused on God's purpose, He ensures your well-being.

Because of the high number of arrests and apprehensions we were experiencing across the country, the sector established an emergency operations center (EOC). This center included various local, state, and federal agencies. A few other managers and I were requested to oversee specific operations for a couple of months to tackle the situation and ensure national security was maintained.

It was an incredibly hectic period for me. I was juggling numerous responsibilities at work, as I needed to keep a close eye on the operations of both the EOC and the teams and units I managed. To make matters more challenging, my mother-in-law passed away during this time, which deeply affected our family. I had to be a source of strength for my wife as we navigated this tough situation together. The church became my refuge, a place where I found solace. While I did spend personal time seeking the Lord, there's something special about coming together for corporate prayer that brought me peace.

I remained an engaged participant in the Peer Support Program, and isn't it remarkable how, during our toughest times, we often find that someone is sent our way to offer support, even amid our own turmoil? I was in my office by myself when a colleague came in to talk. He clearly had much weighing on his mind. Typically, when someone stops by, especially if I sense they're in need of a conversation, I make it a point to silence my phone and focus entirely on them.

I recall thinking, *If only this person understood what I was experiencing.* Yet, I set aside my own selfish concerns and chose to follow God's guidance, focusing on what my friend needed to share. When he started to speak, his words came out slowly, revealing the burden he was carrying. I gently encouraged him, saying, "Take your time. I'm here for you, brother." Suddenly, a wave of emotions poured out from him, reminding me that often it's not just about the words we say but the support we offer that truly matters.

During that season, our agency faced numerous challenges, and emotions ran high. Yet, we supported each other, and that camaraderie truly made a difference. I am grateful to my Lord for the exceptional leadership at HQ during those difficult times; a leader who genuinely cares for their team can profoundly influence the mindset of the group, turning potential defeat into victory. The scripture that deeply resonates with me regarding this type of leadership is Psalm 37:30–31: "The mouths of the righteous utter wisdom, and their tongues speak what is just. The law of their God is in their hearts; their feet do not slip."

As agents, we often bear the weight of expectations; when people see a uniform, they tend to view us as invincible, overlooking the real individuals behind it. Once we return home, we step into various roles—being a parent, a spouse, a sibling, and even a son or daughter. Many of us also engage in community activities, serving as coaches, volunteer chefs, organizers for fundraisers, ministers, Sunday school teachers, and pastors, among other roles. Despite these responsibilities, we remain dedicated to our mission of ensuring national security.

When my friend finished sharing what was on his mind, I realized that he had unknowingly offered me support. We were both navigating similar challenges, and he was also feeling overwhelmed at work. While that was something we had grown accustomed to as part of our agency life, it's the personal struggles that truly weigh us down.

The comforting truth is that during these tough times, our Lord is there, ready to embrace us and provide solace. Yet, too often, we hesitate to approach Him and lay our burdens down. As humans, we tend to think we can handle everything on our own, but in doing so, we often end up causing ourselves more pain.

In Matthew 11:28–30, we are gently reminded by God that He has already made the ultimate sacrifice for both our salvation and our peace. He calls out, "Come to me, all you who are weary and burdened, and I will give you rest. Take my yoke upon you and learn from me, for I am gentle and humble in heart, and you will find rest for your souls. For my yoke is easy and my burden is light." This invitation is not just for the moment of our salvation, but a daily call to seek His peace and comfort in Him.

A TIME OF HEALING

Those who have served as first responders, whether in the military, as medical professionals, firefighters, or law enforcement—from dispatchers to officers on patrol—have all faced profoundly impactful experiences. Often, our loved ones are unaware of the challenges we've encountered. The hesitation to open up likely relates to a piece of wisdom my uncle, a former police officer, once imparted: "Keep work at work and home at home."

Many of us tend to believe that keeping our struggles to

ourselves is the best approach. We often choose not to share our experiences, not out of a desire to exclude our loved ones but rather to protect them from the chaos that surrounds us. Opening up would mean exposing the harsh realities we face. As the years go by, holding everything inside can take a toll, though. We can only bear so much before we reach our breaking point.

In the book of 1 Kings, the prophet Elijah was summoned by God to minister to the nation of Israel during a tumultuous period marked by the reign of a feeble king named Ahab. His wife, the ruthless and ambitious Queen Jezebel, had convinced Ahab to embrace the worship of Baal, leading to the tragic slaughter of many of God's prophets at her orders.

Elijah had achieved a remarkable triumph when he defeated 450 prophets of Baal on Mount Carmel through God's power. Shortly afterward, Jezebel sent a message to Elijah, stating in 1 Kings 19:2, "May the gods deal with me, be it ever so severely, if by this time tomorrow I do not make your life like that of one of them."

Elijah was so terrified by the threat that she would end his life by the next day that he dashed into the wilderness to escape. He was consumed by fear and ran for an entire day. When he finally paused to catch his breath, he found refuge under a tree, and all he could do was pray for the Lord to end his life, feeling utterly exhausted and overwhelmed.

Haven't we all experienced moments like this? Even as Christians, it only takes a small whisper of doubt from the enemy during our struggles to make us feel overwhelmed. How often have we found ourselves praying to God, asking Him to end our pain and bring us home?

Life may not always be easy, as God never promised us that it would be. However, He assured us of His constant presence, just as He was there for Elijah. During a challenging night, God sent the angel of the Lord to Elijah not once, but twice, providing him with nourishment and encouragement for the long journey ahead. Similarly, in our times of need, God often sends messengers to support us. I have found that God brings people into our lives to share His Word, uplift us, and remind us of our purpose and His unwavering love.

Elijah journeyed for forty days and eventually reached Horeb, the mountain of God, where he entered a cave. Overwhelmed by his circumstances, he felt a deep sense of despair and isolation. He was convinced that he was the last remaining prophet, believing that Jezebel had taken the lives of all the others.

Many of us can relate to Elijah's emotions during such a

challenging period. When facing trials, we often feel alone, as if we are the only ones enduring hardship. In 1 Peter 4:12, we find reassurance that our struggles have purpose: "Dear friends, do not be surprised at the fiery ordeal that has come on you to test you, as though something strange were happening to you." Like Elijah, who lost sight of his identity and that God was the one fighting for him, we too can forget where our strength comes from in those moments, which can leave us feeling powerless.

God posed a question to Elijah: "What are you doing here, Elijah?" Elijah felt as if he was fighting an uphill battle, with no hope of triumph. Life can often feel this way; the adversary of our souls excels at making us believe we are alone and that no one cares.

Like Elijah, we sometimes retreat into our own caves, which is precisely what the enemy desires. Being in this state doesn't benefit anyone; the enemy understands that God has given you a unique mission that only you can accomplish, and it's his goal to prevent you from achieving it.

The LORD instructed Elijah to step outside and stand on the mountain, as noted in 1 Kings 19:11–13: As the LORD approached, "a great and powerful wind tore the mountains apart and shattered the rocks before the LORD, but the LORD was not in the wind. After the wind there was an earthquake, but the LORD was not in the earthquake. After the earthquake came a fire, but the LORD was not in the fire." After all these dramatic events, Elijah heard a gentle whisper. When he recognized it, God asked him, "What are you doing here, Elijah?"

What was the Lord revealing to Elijah? I firmly believe the Lord was illustrating the message found in Zechariah 4:6: "Not by might nor by power, but by my Spirit, says the LORD Almighty." God was reminding Elijah that his mission could not be achieved through his own abilities or human strength, but rather through the Spirit of God!

It's wonderful how the Lord brings us back to the core truth; like a caring parent, He reassures and encourages us. Now, *what are you doing here?* In essence, it's time to get moving, rise up, and fulfill the purpose I have set for you! Stop wallowing in self-pity, trust in me, and witness the incredible things I will accomplish through them that trust me!

Elijah still had a purpose, and in the cave, Elijah discovered that God's presence can be gentle. He realized that real strength lies in paying attention to God's soft whispers rather than only focusing on grand acts of power. Elijah found a fresh motivation from God, and even with the threats surrounding him, he decided to follow the Lord's guidance.

Meanwhile, Elijah carried on with his prophetic work, reaching a level where God spoke through him to convey messages to the kings of Israel, confronting their wicked practices.

When we find ourselves in times of trouble, we need to learn to find peace in Him, just as the psalmist expressed in Psalm 23:1–4, "The LORD is my shepherd, I lack nothing. He makes me lie down in green pastures, he leads me beside quiet waters, he refreshes my soul. He guides me along the right paths for his name's sake. Even though I walk through the darkest valley, I will fear no evil, for you are with me; your rod and your staff, they comfort me."

chapter nine

SYSTEMATICALLY

"For God is not a God of disorder but of peace—as in all the congregations of the Lord's people."

1 CORINTHIANS 14:33

Life can often feel chaotic, but it's important to remember that God is a God of order. Even when everything seems disorganized, have faith that He is working to bring everything into alignment. Consider the caterpillar that wraps itself in a cocoon; from the outside, it may appear to be a jumble, yet within, a beautiful transformation is taking place. The caterpillar may not fully grasp the changes happening, but it trusts the journey and patiently awaits its emergence as a butterfly.

A caterpillar cannot grasp the essence of a butterfly until it undergoes its transformation. Similarly, a person who is focused solely on worldly matters, without the influence of the Spirit of God, will struggle to comprehend divine truths. In 2 Corinthians 5:17, we are reminded, "Therefore, if anyone is in Christ, the new creation has come: The old has gone, the new is here!"

This signifies that in Christ, we become a new creation— not merely through religious practices, but through a profound change of the heart. God promises us a new heart, as stated in Ezekiel 36:26, "I will give you a new heart and put a new spirit in you; I will remove from you your heart of stone and give you a heart of flesh."

Before we accept Christ as our Savior, our understanding of spiritual matters is limited. However, when we receive the new spiritual heart mentioned in Ezekiel, we begin to grasp God's ways. He gradually unveils His plan for our lives, revealing it piece by piece. Walking with God is a lifelong journey, and He shares certain truths with us over time rather than all at once. This gradual revelation is for our benefit; just as a butterfly needs time to develop its wings, we too need to grow strong enough to handle the truths we learn. If we were to receive all the truths at once, we might find ourselves overwhelmed and unprepared.

If I had known all the challenges I would face from my time at the academy to becoming a manager in my agency, I might have chosen to walk away before I even began. Similarly, had I been shown the trials I would encounter since I dedicated my life to Him on Highway 44, I might have thought it was too much to bear. Yet, God guides us from one level of glory to another, as stated in 2 Corinthians 3:18. This journey is a transformative process, leading us to reflect the image of Christ.

During our time at the K9 handler academy, one of the key lessons emphasized was the importance of conducting area searches systematically with our K9s. To ensure we didn't overlook anything during our sweeps, we were taught specific patterns that needed to be followed thoroughly. Initially, the system felt a bit clumsy, but as we practiced, it gradually became second nature to us. The more we engaged in this process, the more comfortable and proficient we became.

We understood that adhering to these patterns ensured we wouldn't overlook anything. This approach instilled confidence in us, as we were certain we had completed our tasks meticulously and relied on our K9 partners to perform theirs effectively, leading to a thoroughly searched area where nothing was overlooked.

We understand, both from the scriptures and our own experiences, that the God of the Bible is a faithful and orderly God who does not act randomly. Everything that happens in our lives, as we strive to live righteously, has a specific reason and purpose. This knowledge gives us assurance that the challenges we face are part of a divine plan and will ultimately lead to glorifying the Lord in various ways.

As long as we adhere to the principles we were taught as K9 handlers, when that voice of doubt tries to undermine us by suggesting we have overlooked a find in our search area, we can have inner peace and assertively say, "Get behind me, Satan. I know in whom I trust."

AT HIS TIME

Believing that God is a God of order rather than chaos can greatly influence how we handle the trials and challenges we face. In today's fast-paced technological world, we've grown used to instant gratification. If we desire something, a few clicks online can have it delivered to our doorstep within a couple of days.

I was raised in an era where watching cartoons meant waiting for Saturday mornings or tuning in on weekdays at 3:30 p.m. right after school. Nowadays, kids can simply switch on the TV and pick whatever they want to stream, enjoying instant access to cartoons. I think this has fostered a sense of entitlement in many of us, as we've lost the experience of waiting for something we want.

Waiting can be a valuable experience, as it allows us to truly value what we have longed for. I genuinely feel that the extended journey to my promotions fostered a profound appreciation for those roles, ultimately shaping me into a more effective leader. Similarly, our path to parenthood took time, which not only deepened our love for our children but also enhanced our appreciation for other kids in ways we might not have experienced otherwise. Even after all these years, my wife and I continue to be involved in a children's ministry at our church, reflecting that enduring gratitude.

Trust me, when God asks you to wait, don't view it as a negative experience. In fact, it's often for your own good. I remember when I was a child, I desperately wanted a Huffy bike, which was the most sought-after brand back then. My neighbor had one for sale, but it was quite pricey. I had my heart set on it for my birthday, but when the day came, I didn't get it and was left disappointed. My dad reassured me to be patient, saying he had a plan for when I would receive it. As the months passed, I began to think he had completely forgotten about the bike.

That Christmas, my dad and uncle wanted to create a truly memorable experience for us. As all the cousins gathered inside, they orchestrated something incredibly special. Somehow, they managed to climb onto the roof of my grandmother's house and began stomping around with Christmas bells. At that age, we all still believed in Santa Claus, and when we heard those jingle sounds, our excitement soared; we were convinced that Santa had arrived, and nothing could change our minds. As we rushed outside to see what was happening, someone shouted, "Look up at the roof!" To our amazement, we spotted all the gifts up there, except for mine. As we continued to search the area, we stumbled upon a large cardboard box. My heart raced as I thought, *Could it be my bike?*

While we were checking out the box, I was thrilled to see my name on it. I'll always remember the excitement I felt when I opened it, only to find something even better than the bike I had wished for! It was the same brand, but a more premium model, and it was completely new! I can still picture the night we got home; my dad and I worked together to assemble it. Sure, he did most of the heavy lifting, but it was a memorable project for me. My dad stayed up late with me, and by the time we finally went to bed, it was nearly six in the morning.

I later discovered that my dad had managed to buy the bike at a fantastic price! That experience taught me to always trust my father; when he said "not now," it wasn't out of meanness but for a good reason. I vividly remember the day I woke up and dashed out the front door, riding my shiny new bike around the neighborhood. It was an incredible feeling! Waiting for that moment helped me appreciate the things I received even more.

I think that when we fully embrace a waiting period, it can bring about a transformation within that is far more valuable than anything money can purchase. Personally, waiting has instilled in me a sense of strength, maturity, and humility that I couldn't have gained in any other way. God has His own timing, which often doesn't align with ours, but if we can learn to trust and accept His timing, I assure you it will lead to unexpected blessings.

When we reach out to God in prayer, we can expect our requests to be answered in three distinct ways: a quick yes, a wait, or a no. Everyone enjoys the quick yeses—those moments when everything falls into place, and the answer seems to arrive the moment you say amen. Then there are the waiting periods, which can be tough but ultimately help us develop a strength we might not have discovered otherwise. These answers are often less popular among us. Last, there are the no answers. You'll know when God closes a door, and while it's not something anyone relishes, these moments are crucial for our spiritual growth. As I reflect now in my later years, I can see how many times unanswered prayers protected me from paths that would have led to less favorable outcomes.

A caring parent understands what their child truly needs, just as God understands what is best for His children. One of the toughest lessons I faced as both a parent and a leader was learning to say no. Even though the child or those under my care might not have seen it then, I was always acting in their best interest. God knows the right timing; He won't let us emerge from our cocoon too soon, as that would cause more harm than good. Our role is to have faith in His ways, even when things appear challenging—His plan is always the best one.

CHRYSALIS

I have come to understand that thriving in the midst of chaos is not solely due to my own abilities or identity, but rather because of the strength and love of God. Being a follower of Christ doesn't mean we are simply automatons following orders from a distant deity. This is a misunderstanding that those who haven't experienced a personal relationship with God often feel. He is a compassionate God who wants us to flourish in every aspect of our lives. As we grow and succeed, we bring more honor to Him. Ultimately, we realize that our actions are meant to glorify God rather than earn the approval of others, and through our faithfulness, we can also bring blessings to those around us.

Paul the apostle addressed this topic in 2 Corinthians 4:7–9, 15–18: "But we have this treasure in jars of clay to show that this all-surpassing power is from God and not from us. We are hard pressed on every side, but not crushed; perplexed, but not in despair; persecuted, but not abandoned; struck down, but not destroyed. All this is for your benefit, so that the grace that is reaching more and more people may cause thanksgiving to overflow to the glory of God.

"Therefore we do not lose heart. Though outwardly we are wasting away, yet inwardly we are being renewed day by day. For our light and momentary troubles are achieving for us an eternal glory that far outweighs them all. So we fix our eyes not on what is seen, but on what is unseen, since what is seen is temporary, but what is unseen is eternal."

As we stay committed to our divine purpose, God will manage the distractions that surround us. Whether at work, home, or even at church, there will always be forces trying to disrupt our focus. Just as a butterfly emerges from its chrysalis, gaining strength to spread its wings and soar, God strengthens us through the challenges we encounter as Christians.

Stay dedicated to your journey; in time, God will guide you through. He always equips you for what lies ahead. Keep your faith strong in every aspect of your life, whether at work or with your loved ones. In His perfect timing, everything will fall into place. It may be hard to recognize during the difficult moments, but if you persist in your efforts and trust in what you cannot yet see, victory will be yours. God is leading us toward triumph, forged through our challenges, and that cannot be taken from you.

CHANGE IS GOOD

As a country, we were approaching an election year, and our agency was in need of a transformation. I sensed a collective hope for a positive shift. The workload was relentless, and we were operating with fewer agents than needed. Our teams were exhausted, and families were feeling the absence of their loved ones. We had seen some of the highest seizures and apprehension numbers in years, but clearly a change was necessary. After enduring eight challenging years, we simply couldn't face another four years of the same struggles.

With arrests and apprehensions continually on the rise everywhere and a shortage of staff, everyone found themselves juggling multiple roles both in the field and at headquarters. Many upper management members had been assigned to Washington, DC, and other locations across the country. This situation allowed managers and supervisors at the local level to temporarily step up into higher positions.

I was invited to take on a higher upper management role for nearly a year. During that period, I had the chance to engage with our specialty programs, which allowed me to collaborate once more with the K9 units at the headquarters level. In addition to overseeing the K9 units, I also managed the horse patrol units, boat patrol units, and various other programs within our division.

Even though it was a hectic time for everyone, I truly appreciated where the Lord had placed me in my career. Each morning, without exception, I would arrive early at my office and start my day with prayer. I prayed for the nation, for our leaders, for our agents and their families, and for all the employees at our sector.

At this level, people generally maintained their distance from one another. I found myself longing for the morning meetings with my teams. While upper management still met several times a week, these meetings felt quite different from what I was used to. The team meetings I was accustomed to had a more personal touch, likely because we had faced so many challenges together, which brought us closer to one another.

This experience allowed me to see things from a different perspective. While the decisions I faced were on a larger scale, the core principle remained the same: prioritize the well-being of your team. I believe that the Lord prepares us for what lies ahead, and I am sincerely thankful for the remarkable leaders who guided me with their wisdom throughout the years. During the toughest moments, I found myself drawing on the lessons they had imparted.

One morning, my division chief summoned me to his office and inquired whether the horse patrol could be prepared to deploy on short notice. Since I received daily updates on the status of all units in our programs, I was aware that the team was more than equipped for the task. He instructed me to ensure that a small group of men and their horses were ready to deploy, as they would be representing our sector at the inauguration parade of President Elect Donald J. Trump.

A close friend of mine, who is also a manager, took charge of the team during the inauguration. It was a tremendous honor for all of us to participate in this significant event; we could all sense that positive changes were on the horizon. The passage that perfectly captures what our nation was on the brink of experiencing and what it had just experienced, is from Proverbs 29:2: "When the righteous thrive, the people rejoice; when the wicked rule, the people groan."

On inauguration day, every law enforcement agency from across the country was in attendance. We felt immense pride as we watched our team march by and salute the new president of the United States. It was heartwarming to see the pride and honor on the president's face as he returned the salute. At last, hope, honor, and pride had been restored to the White House, led by a president who valued God, country, and family.

HUNDE AUS LAUFEN

In the world of K9 training, there comes a moment when you simply need to allow a dog to be a dog. The instructors at the K9 handler academy referred to this concept with a German term, *Hunde aus Laufen*, which translates to "dogs out running." Our K9 facility featured a spacious outdoor area where we could let our dogs roam and enjoy their time as dogs.

Typically, we would let three to four dogs out at once in this expansive run.

There's truly nothing like witnessing these dogs in their element; their interactions with each other are simply heartwarming. While they are all business when on duty, watching them play and frolic like young pups is a joy to behold. Seeing a dog confined to a chain or a cage for most of their life is heartbreaking. The sadness etched on a dog's face in such circumstances is unmistakable and deeply troubling.

I have genuinely observed both of these situations within the people of our agency as well. During certain moments, morale hit rock bottom, and despite management's efforts, the team just couldn't bounce back. This was often due to a shortage of manpower and poor policies from DC that left us feeling restricted as an agency. On the flip side, I've also seen times when agents were equipped and empowered to do their jobs, and the outcomes were incredible.

As agents, we understood that our primary responsibility remained unchanged regardless of who was in charge or which administration occupied the White House. Our strong sense of camaraderie compelled us to fulfill our duties without exception.

Christians are encouraged to spread the hope that resides

within, especially in places where hope seems absent. Our hope stems from the understanding that God is in control and guides our lives. Many people feel hopeless, which causes their emotions to be unstable, much like waves in the sea. However, we are not among those who are easily swayed; we know where our hope lies, and we will not lose heart. As stated in Hebrews 10:23, "Let us hold unswervingly to the hope we profess, for he who promised is faithful."

The agency has consistently shown its commitment to supporting agents and their families through various resiliency initiatives. I had the privilege of participating in the early stages of the Veterans Support Program, a national initiative designed to aid all veterans within our agency. This program provides valuable resources related to employment benefits, as well as mental, physical, and emotional health support.

Two years beyond the new administration taking charge, the sector was seeing a notable decrease in criminal activity. This shift provided me the opportunity to get involved with the Veterans Support Program.

As a Marine Corps veteran, I understood the complexities surrounding disability claims. I was eager to start the training, which was outstanding; it included information on how to buy back military service time and explored services related to survivor and dependent benefits, along with other important topics for veterans. This program allowed us to assist our fellow veterans, and I truly felt a sense of accomplishment in taking part in this new initiative.

We had genuinely experienced a period of grace; the economy was thriving, and people could finally enjoy a better quality of life. There was a renewed sense of patriotism across the country, and things were looking up.

Wearing the uniform felt rewarding once more. After enduring eight years under the previous administration, which felt like a dark period for our nation, the shift was refreshing. It felt like we were emerging from a time when, as the Bible mentions, people were calling evil good, and good evil.

Just as we started to see a glimmer of hope, the entire world faced an extraordinary wave of grief. The arrival of COVID-19 caught us all off guard. This pandemic was unlike anything we had ever encountered. It changed every aspect of our lives, from how we connected with others to our financial situations, the economy, our shopping habits, education, work routines, dining experiences, and even our mental, emotional, and spiritual well-being.

This pandemic felt like it had come right from the depths of hell. Countless individuals were too frightened to step outside their doors; a pervasive sense of fear gripped the community. Numerous businesses and places of worship were forced to shut their doors.

Being a Christian does not shield us from difficulties; in fact, our Lord Himself cautioned us about the inevitability of trials. In John 16:33, He reassures us, saying, "I have told you these things, so that in me you may have peace. In this world you will have trouble. But take heart! I have overcome the world." When Jesus proclaimed, "I have overcome the world," He was declaring His triumph over the forces of evil, sin, and death through His sacrifice on the cross and His resurrection.

This victory signifies the defeat of Satan's influence and the corrupting powers of the world, providing believers with the hope that, through faith in Him, they too can rise above the challenges they face.

chapter ten

STEPPING STONE

"And we know that in all things God works for the good of those who love him, who have been called according to his purpose."

ROMANS 8:28

Life's challenges are a part of our journey. It's been said that we are either entering a trial, facing one, or emerging from it. These hardships can manifest in various ways, such as the loss of a loved one, health issues, financial struggles, setbacks in our careers, job loss, or family conflicts.

Hardships can be incredibly tough to navigate, but the real question is how you will choose to respond to them. Will you permit this trial to become a stumbling block in your path, or will you use it as a stepping stone, as an opportunity to progress? The Bible encourages us to see challenges as opportunities for growth rather than obstacles. Facing difficulties with faith can lead to spiritual development, perseverance, and maturity. As stated in James 1:2–4, "Consider it pure joy, my brothers and sisters, whenever you face trials of many kinds, because you know that the testing of your faith produces perseverance. Let perseverance finish its work so that you may be mature and complete, not lacking anything."

In challenging moments, the words our instructors shared hit home more than ever: "It's not a matter of if you'll get bitten, but when?" In life, we are faced with many detours; how we approach them is the true test. Will you choose to give up and miss out on your potential? Or will you press on, overcoming obstacles, and embrace the purpose you were meant to achieve?

As dog handlers, we were aware that a bite was inevitable, but when one actually occurred, it often turned out to be manageable. Sure, it stung, and some bites can be quite severe, but the real question is whether you'll keep pushing forward. I've observed individuals who get a minor nip and decide to steer clear of dogs forever, while others endure much worse injuries with significant damage, yet they persist without hesitation. The same applies to life's challenges; I've seen people give up after just a gentle nudge from adversity, while others display incredible resilience, facing their trials with a strength that is truly inspiring.

WILL YOU PERSEVERE?

In the Bible is a powerful story about a man named Job who faced numerous challenges and hardships, ultimately losing everything he held dear. Despite these overwhelming trials, Job maintained his faith in God. In Job 1:1, Job is portrayed as a blameless and righteous individual who revered God and turned away from wrongdoing. His deep relationship with God ensured that everything Job undertook or possessed thrived though divine favor.

One day, the angels gathered with Satan to present themselves before the Lord. "The LORD said to Satan, 'Where have you come from?' Satan answered the LORD, 'From roaming throughout the earth, going back and forth on it'" (Job 1:7). Essentially, Satan had been searching everywhere for someone to tempt. The Lord then asked if he had considered

His servant Job. Satan answered that because of the Lord's protection over Job, he was unable to harm him. Satan claimed that if that protection were lifted, Job would surely curse God. God then granted Satan permission to test Job.

Job experienced a series of devastating losses. First, raiders took away his oxen, donkeys, camels, and killed his servants. Then, a fire from the sky destroyed his sheep. The final blow came when a powerful wind struck the house where all his children were gathered for a celebration, causing it to collapse on them.

Despite these tragedies, Job maintained his faith in God. He expressed, "Naked I came from my mother's womb, and naked shall I return there. The LORD gave, and the LORD has taken away; Blessed be the name of the LORD" (ESV). The scripture notes in Job 1:22 that through all of this, Job did not sin or blame God.

Job faced an unimaginable tragedy with the loss of his children and his possessions. In the midst of his suffering, Satan afflicted his health with excruciating boils that covered his body from head to toe. To make matters worse, his wife, in her own despair, questioned his steadfastness, urging him to abandon his integrity, saying, "Are you still holding on to your principles? Curse God and die!" (GW).

Job's friends, despite their intentions to console him, ended up blaming him for sinning against God. They urged him to seek forgiveness for his mistakes, hoping that it would restore God's blessings in his life. Instead of offering genuine support, they started to doubt Job's connection with God and criticized his character. Their guidance stemmed from their personal beliefs and perspectives, rather than truly trusting in Job and being there for him.

We often feel isolated during our toughest moments, even from those we hold dear. This experience can be painful, as the very people who should understand us often don't. The adversary seeks to exploit our vulnerability, aiming to shake our faith to its core. His intention is to lead us to doubt God, knowing that this can set off a chain reaction that affects not only us but also those around us.

Job's sincere repentance and prayer for his friends led to a remarkable transformation in his life. God not only restored his health and possessions but blessed him with double what he had previously, effectively healing him and bringing his life back to a flourishing state, as noted in Job 42.

If everything you cherished was stripped away, would your faith in God remain intact? This is a challenging question, one that may leave us pondering deeply. Only through His presence could we navigate such profound loss. In Him, we find the resilience to hold on, and through the Spirit of God we draw the strength to persevere on our journey with Him.

HANGING UP THE LEASH

The impact of COVID-19 transformed our world, our nation, our organization, and each of us in profound ways. Over time, what once felt unusual became our new reality. We adapted to the heartache of losing loved ones, the daily routine of wearing masks, and the constant presence of hand sanitizers. Isolation became a shared experience, our children transitioned to home schooling, and we found new ways to connect with our loved ones through online gatherings and virtual worship. All of these changes, once so foreign, gradually became part of our everyday lives.

During those challenging times, food and essential supplies were hard to come by, and the pressure from the government and various organizations to receive vaccines only heightened the anxiety. For some, these struggles brought them closer to their faith, while others turned away from any connection to God. It was a frightening period that felt like a turning point, leaving many to wonder if life would ever return to what it once was—and in many ways, it truly hasn't.

No matter where you turned, the atmosphere was

unsettling; whether you were driving or shopping, the streets felt deserted. Work life had shifted dramatically as well. Those deemed nonessential were instructed to work from home, while essential workers continued to report to their jobs each day. Many chose to isolate themselves in their offices, and social interactions became scarce, creating an even greater challenge for everyone involved.

This period truly challenged us all, and during those days, my prayer life increased significantly. I recall having conversations with God, expressing my confusion about the struggles we faced, yet affirming my trust in Him. I asked for guidance on how to navigate through this difficult time. Despite my own fears and uncertainties about the future, the Lord inspired me to offer comfort to others in their moments of need.

Roughly a year later, things began to calm down at work somewhat. By that time, nonessential personnel were invited to return, and everyone had adjusted to the new normal. We remained focused on our mission to ensure that national security was upheld at its highest level.

One morning, a close friend of mine stopped by my office for a chat. He inquired about how much longer I had until I could retire. I replied that I had been eligible for retirement for the past six months. He looked at me like I was crazy and asked if I had thought about the monthly annuity amount difference if I retired now instead of waiting for mandatory retirement. I admitted that I hadn't thought about it. Once more, he looked at me strange and questioned why I hadn't.

He took out a piece of paper, asked me a few questions, and started crunching some numbers. A few minutes later, he presented me with the results. He explained, "This is what you would receive each month if you chose to retire tomorrow, and this is the amount you'd get if you waited until the mandatory retirement age." Then, with a serious expression, he asked, "Are you really considering staying for another seven years just to earn an extra hundred dollars a month?"

He continued questioning the need to wait when one could retire at such a young age. If I chose to, I wouldn't need to work at all. However, many retirees opt for part-time contract work, allowing them to spend the majority of their time with family and pursuing their hobbies. My friend certainly made a compelling case that day.

I have to admit, I hadn't given much thought to retirement, but what my friend said clicked for me then. I realized that I had never considered retirement in that way before. When I got home that day, I sat down for a heartfelt conversation with my wife. I asked her to join me in prayer, as making this decision was quite challenging for anyone.

After spending a few weeks doing research and making phone calls, I finally felt ready to take a leap of faith and hang up the leash. I submitted my retirement request to our human resources team. It was a bittersweet moment for me. On one hand, I was excited about the new chapter ahead, but on the other, I felt a twinge of sadness because this job had been such a significant part of my life for many years.

After I submitted my retirement packet, everything seemed to move quickly. Through my prayer life, I sensed a profound guidance from the Lord, affirming that this was the right decision for me. Many people were surprised that I was actually going through with it. A common question I faced during this time was whether I thought I would miss working.

I'm grateful that I created a life for myself outside my career. Unlike my experience when I left the Marines, this transition didn't feel as painful. I've come to understand that back then the Marines were my entire world; they took precedence over my family and even my faith. At one time, my career in law enforcement held that same significance.

When I fully dedicated my life to Christ and made Him the focal point of my existence, I came to understand that my priorities had been out of order. Now, regardless of where I am or what I'm doing, I find my contentment in Him. This is the essence of our peace; as long as anything or anyone else occupies the space in our hearts meant for our Lord, true contentment will elude us.

Without Christ in our lives, we often find ourselves chasing after the next promotion, the next career milestone, the next thrill, a new relationship, or the latest gadget—the list never seems to end. The apostle Paul captures this sentiment in Philippians 4:11–13, where he shares, "I am not saying this because I am in need, for I have learned to be content whatever the circumstances. I know what it is to be in need, and I know what it is to have plenty. I have learned the secret of being content in any and every situation, whether well fed or hungry, whether living in plenty or in *want*. I can do all this through him who gives me strength."

My retirement celebration was quite a pleasant experience. My friends organized a lovely luncheon for me and presented me with several cherished gifts that I truly value, especially since they came from them. I am grateful to God every single day for these wonderful friends. When anyone inquires if I miss my job, I always respond that I miss the people.

ANOTHER TRIAL

A year after my retirement, my wife and I fell seriously ill with COVID-19. Surprisingly, we had managed to stay healthy during the height of the pandemic, but eventually, the virus found its way to us. I was fortunate to recover relatively quickly, but my wife struggled significantly. She moved from one emergency room to another, desperately seeking relief, but her condition just wouldn't get better.

During this period, we discovered that she had diabetes, which complicated matters even more. Eventually, my wife managed to recover from COVID-19, but her body was never the same. While we were both treated with antibiotics for our COVID symptoms, her underlying condition led to an allergic reaction to the medication.

It had been an incredibly challenging year. My wife visited countless doctors, yet her health was not improving. This entire ordeal felt far from ordinary, more like a spiritual battle. My wife lost so much weight that she became unrecognizable. Eating and sleeping became difficult for her; she could only manage to sleep for two to three hours at a stretch. Her situation became so dire that she even said her goodbyes to me.

One afternoon, as I was focused on my work, my wife

approached me in tears. With a heavy heart, she shared her thoughts about what I should do if she were to leave us soon. She had taken the time to write letters for each of our boys, as well as one for me, and she gently pointed out where she had placed them, in case she would be joining our heavenly Father soon. Even though I was at a loss for words, I did my utmost to reassure her that everything was going to be fine. Inside, I felt as if my world had just been shattered. This was an incredibly tough moment for both of us.

One evening, after completing a temporary contract job out of town, I received a call from my wife. She informed me that her sister was taking her to urgent care. She reassured me not to worry, explaining that she just needed to get some fluids through an IV. She also asked if I could swing by the house to grab her purse, which she had forgotten. As I drove home, I noticed her car parked in the driveway. Upon entering the house, I saw her purse sitting on the kitchen island. The weight of reality struck me as soon as I walked through the door. I had been trying so hard to stay strong for her and the kids, but in that instant, everything came crashing down. I found myself crying more deeply than I ever had before, overwhelmed by a sense of emptiness that I felt in the house.

I envisioned a future without her by my side. I realized I

had been in denial about my wife's condition, constructing barriers around myself to shield my heart. Suddenly, God shattered those walls with incredible force. After pouring out my heart in prayer, I sensed my Father's hand reassuring me that everything was going to be fine.

I could see how hard my wife was trying to maintain a sense of normalcy for the sake of our boys, but deep down, I knew she was struggling every single day. We turned to prayer and sought support from others, yet nothing was improving; in fact, things seemed to be getting more difficult.

These moments truly reveal the state of our spiritual condition. Psalm 1:3 illustrates the fruit of having a genuine relationship with the Lord: "That person is like a tree planted by streams of water, which yields its fruit in season and whose leaf does not wither—whatever they do prospers." I've come to understand that you shouldn't wait for challenges to draw closer to God; nurturing that relationship beforehand is what will carry you through the storms of life.

Then, out of nowhere, we turned the corner—just as suddenly as the illness had struck, my wife's healing arrived. She had been fighting sickness for nearly two years. We discovered that her body was essentially shutting down because of the allergic reaction to the antibiotics, and it took that long for her to recover. We are truly thankful to our Lord for being merciful and answering our prayers.

Those who have experienced a situation like this understand how profoundly it can alter your life. My wife and I gained invaluable insights from this challenging journey. Prior to this experience, despite our dedicated service to the Lord and our commitment to living for Him, we often overlooked the blessings around us. We realized that we had been taking our children, our relationship, and even our faith for granted.

God has a unique way of allowing circumstances in our lives that will humble us, but these experiences are not intended to harm us. Instead, they serve a purpose for our growth and development. Reflecting on the hardships I've faced, I realize that, despite their difficulty, I am grateful for each one. They have shaped me into a better person, and I truly believe that these trials were part of a divine plan to bring me closer to Him.

It was truly inspiring to witness my wife's selflessness throughout this challenging time. Even on her toughest days, she found the strength to support others. Such compassion can only come from a deep connection with the Spirit of God. The ability to think of others, even when we are struggling ourselves, is a testament to the time we spend in His presence. This beautifully showcases the essence of who He is.

One of the most profound moments in the gospels occurs when Jesus is on the cross, facing His own death, yet he still shows deep compassion for His mother, Mary. In that heart-wrenching moment, He looks at her and then at John, saying, "Woman, here is your son," and to John, "Here is your mother." From that moment forward, John welcomed Mary into his home (John 19:26–27). This demonstrates the strength of love and care even in the darkest times.

GOD IS NOT DONE WITH YOU

What comes next? This question lingered in my mind after I retired. While I had been preoccupied with concerns for my wife during her illness, I was also grappling with my own internal conflict. I found myself wrestling with my sense of self; retirement had stripped away my identity. For so long, I had defined myself by my uniform, my badge, and my gun. Without my role and title, I felt adrift, uncertain of who I truly was.

Even though I understood my identity in Him and recognized the purpose He had set for me, I still felt unsettled. I realized that to move forward in triumph, I needed to be truthful with myself and fully surrender everything once more.

One Sunday morning, as the pastor invited those seeking salvation or prayer to come forward, I made a personal decision to lay everything down at the altar. I felt a strong sense of His presence surrounding me. I repented and asked the Lord to forgive me for what I had made my life all about.

In that instant, I experienced once again that profound peace that surpasses all understanding. We often reclaim what we've placed on the altar, whether it's unforgiveness, pride, selfishness, doubt, or anything else that the enemy throws our way. Often, we don't realize that these things can establish a stronghold in our lives, preventing us from fully committing to our Lord.

Not long after I approached the altar, I sensed a renewed passion igniting within me. I felt a deep craving for His Word that I hadn't felt since those early moments when I dedicated my life on Highway 44. I was insatiable, eager to absorb and share everything I could. Those rivers of living water were bubbling up inside me once more.

On a Friday afternoon, while I was praying in my living room to prepare for a small group Bible study that we were hosting that evening, I felt a message from the Lord come to me.

While engaged in prayer, I often find myself walking

around, and during one of those moments, my gaze fell upon some memorabilia from my military and law enforcement days displayed in a case. In that instant, I clearly heard a voice reassuring me, saying, "This isn't the end; I still have plans for you. This is merely the start of what you are meant to achieve!" It brought to mind the story of the prophet Elijah, who, feeling despondent, sought refuge in a cave, where the Lord gently asked him, "What are you doing here, Elijah?"

The Lord frequently gives us the freedom to choose our path. We can decide to stay in that cave, becoming like the Dead Sea—filled with incoming water but lacking any outlets, leading to stagnation. Alternatively, we can choose to be like the Jordan River, a source of flowing water that brings life to those around us. Through our obedience, we have the power to nourish and uplift others.

One of the things I truly miss about going to work is the opportunity to connect with people on a personal level. As a chaplain and peer support member, I was blessed with the chance to share the gospel and offer hope to many individuals. While I continue to minister at my church and engage in various ministries, there's a unique and special experience that comes from having one-on-one conversations about God.

When my sons were little, I frequently shared bedtime

stories with them, weaving in Bible verses to create a devotional that connected to their current experiences. I crafted all sorts of unique characters that resonated with them, and they really enjoyed it. My wife often encouraged me to write a book to share these stories with other kids, and I would chuckle and say, "Me? Write a book? No way!"

Time went on, and one evening as I was settling down for bed, I heard His voice again, saying, "It is time." Playfully, I asked, "Time for what, Lord?" Deep down, I understood perfectly what He meant. So, I got to work on my first children's book. I had jotted down some notes from the stories I used to share with my kids when they were little. Remarkably, I completed that book in just three days. I still recall showing the manuscript to my wife, and her reaction was, "Who writes a book in three days?"

The moment I started writing, the onslaught of attacks began. It was as if everything that could possibly go wrong, did. Our washing machine gave out, my son's laptop malfunctioned, our pony suffered an injury and lost an eye, my wife was involved in a car accident, my truck broke down, my contract work slowed down to nothing, and even our pets faced their own troubles. It felt like the instant we chose to share the Word of God to other families through our books, a deluge of difficulties was unleashed on our family.

Even in the face of opposition, we pressed on with our building efforts, much like Nehemiah, and chose to place our trust in God. This commitment led me to write and publish a second children's book that includes scripture to support kids through their challenges.

It has been a wonderful blessing to share these books with others, and we were pleasantly surprised by the positive response and the impact our dedication has made. The term *ministry* signifies service, and it truly reflects our mission to serve others.

Our Lord Jesus, being God incarnate, chose not to seek service for Himself. Instead, He took on the role of a servant, dedicating His life as a sacrifice for many, as stated in Mark 10:45.

On the night He was betrayed, just before the agony of the cross, His thoughts were not on His own suffering but on His disciples. Jesus was fully aware of the trials that lay ahead, the pain and anguish He would face. Yet rather than dwelling on His own fate, He was ready to exemplify the essence of true love for others.

In John 13:4–5, we see Jesus taking on the role of the lowest servant in the household. "He got up from the meal, took off his outer clothing, and wrapped a towel around his waist. After that, he poured water into a basin and began to wash his disciples' feet, drying them with the towel that was wrapped around him." This act was a profound expression of His love, demonstrating his commitment to His disciples until the very end. Even though they were about to betray him and abandon him, Jesus continued to love them deeply.

Throughout my journey with the Lord, I've come to understand a profound truth: Our hope and healing emerge when we support others. It's easy to become sidetracked by the allure of superficial pursuits, and even our challenges can divert us from our true calling. Ultimately, what will truly matter at the end of our journey isn't the wealth we've accumulated or the accomplishments we've achieved. The crucial question will be whether we fully surrendered our lives to Him and earnestly sought Him with all our hearts. As Matthew 6:33 reminds us, "But seek first his kingdom and his righteousness, and all these things will be given to you as well."

About The Author

David Mendoza III is a dedicated servant leader with a rich tapestry of experience spanning faith, service, and storytelling. Holding a seminary degree in biblical studies, he brings a deep understanding of faith and scripture to his work. A retired federal law enforcement officer with over thirty years of service, David has dedicated his life to protecting and serving others. His military background as a Marine Corps veteran further underscores his commitment to duty and resilience.

David's passion for helping others extends beyond his professional life. He has served as a law enforcement chaplain, a peer support member, and a Veterans Support Program volunteer, offering guidance and support to those in need. Currently, David is a Christian minister and former pastor, sharing his faith and wisdom through his ministry. He is also the author of two engaging children's books, *The Biblical Adventures of Floppy and Hoppy* and *Gideon the Brave Bulldog*, which bring biblical stories to life for young readers.

David's life is a testament to the power of faith, service, and storytelling. He is a devoted husband of over thirty years, a father of two boys, and an active member of his church community, where he and his wife are deeply involved in adult and children's ministry, serving as Sunday school teachers, Royal Rangers Commanders, and home Bible group leaders. David's unwavering commitment to helping others, sharing his testimony, and offering support during times of need makes him a true inspiration.

David is reachable via email at *authordavidmendozaiii@yahoo.com* or you can visit his website at *www.booksforhisglory.com* to get in touch.

Unleashed Redemption
A K9 Handler's Story of Hope & Healing

www.ingramcontent.com/pod-product-compliance
Lightning Source LLC
Chambersburg PA
CBHW060927120626
46557CB00003B/905

* 9 7 9 8 9 9 9 1 5 1 5 1 6 0 *